TEACH
YOURSELF
TO BUILD

TEACH YOURSELF TO BUILD

Edward Allen
and Gale Beth Goldberg

The MIT Press
Cambridge, Massachusetts, and London, England

Library of Congress Cataloging in Publication Data

Allen, Edward, 1938-
   Teach yourself to build.

      1. Building-- Amateurs' manuals. I. Goldberg, Gale Beth, joint author. II. Title.
TH148. A63   690   78-21011
ISBN   0-262-51020-0   (paperback edition)
         0-262-51021-9   (student paperback edition)

TABLE OF CONTENTS

MASONRY

STEEL FRAME

CONCRETE FRAME

TEACH
YOURSELF
TO BUILD

GETTING STARTED WITH THE EXERCISES

The purpose of the process of architectural design is to make dreams into built reality. The idea of the exercises contained in this book is to help you become proficient in the most difficult and crucial part of this process, the translation of ideas about architectural form into actual building materials and building processes. This is a book which will help you to learn to make dreams come true.

Architectural dreams undergo their first transformations toward reality in the form of freehand drawings. Freehand drawing is quick, easy, and expressive as compared with mechanical drawing, and it is therefore the major tool of the designer. These exercises will show you how easy and useful it is to do freehand drawings of buildings. All you need is an ordinary pencil and an eagerness to get on with the work.

Do your work directly on the pages of the book. By this means you will bring the book to life, make it uniquely your own, and develop it into a reference book that you will want to consult again and again in the future.

Often the blank spaces which are left for your drawings in the book are very small. This is intentional. A small drawing is easier and faster to do than a larger one. Also, in a small drawing only the essentials can be shown, and the non-essentials must be left out.

When drawing, make a single, decisive pencil stroke for each line. Don't scribble back and forth, and don't attempt to make each line perfect by drawing it too slowly and carefully. Your lines will not be perfectly straight, but it doesn't matter. Your ideas will still be clearly expressed, and that is the point of your work. The freehand communication of ideas about building should become as easy and natural for you as writing a letter to a friend.

You will sometimes be asked to draw freehand, but to a given scale. This is not so odd nor so difficult as it might seem. Where a scale is given next to an exercise, place the edge of a card or a slip of scratch paper against the scale, and make the card into a scale to use in your drawing:

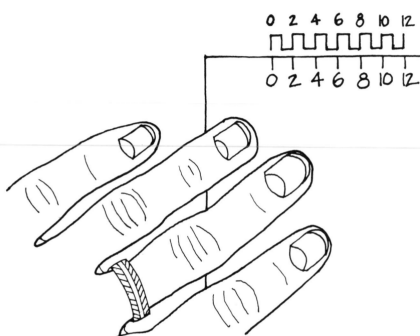

When making the drawing, use the scale you have made to lay off the correct dimensions for your drawing, but don't use it as a straight edge. Continue to draw each line freehand. You will find it remarkably easy and quick to construct scale drawings without instruments, just holding a pencil in one hand and a scale in the other. This is how most architects work in the early and intermediate stages of design.

You will also be asked to draw small "thumbnail" perspectives. Perspectives are useful to the architect because they show more than one side of a building at once, and because they can be made to resemble very closely the way in which a building will actually be perceived. For your purposes here, the accuracy of your perspectives matters very little. Any sort of simple drawing which shows two or more sides of the building at once will be fine.

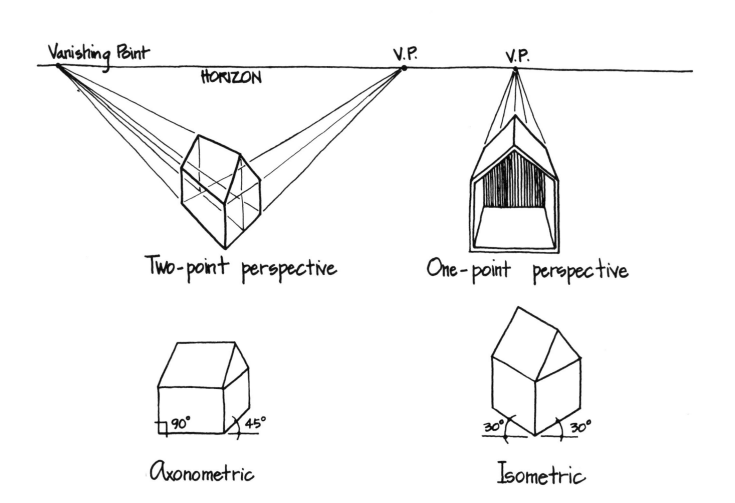

Two-point perspective

One-point perspective

Axonometric 90° 45°

Isometric 30° 30°

This book is not self-sufficient. Most of the exercises will require that you have access to various textbooks on construction. Some suggested references are:

Wood-frame construction: Albert G.H. Dietz. _Dwelling House Construction_, Fourth Edition. Cambridge, M.I.T. Press, 1974.

Masonry and concrete construction: U.S. Department of the Army. _Concrete, Masonry, and Brickwork_, New York, Dover Publications. 1975.

Steel-frame construction: American Institute of Steel Construction. _Manual of Steel Construction_. New York, A.I.S.C., current edition.

General reference: Ramsey and Sleeper. _Architectural Graphic Standards_, New York, John Wiley and Sons. 1970. 3

A WARNING ABOUT STRUCTURAL RULES-OF-THUMB

Structural "rules-of-thumb" are presented at a number of points in this book to enable the reader to proceed readily with the exercises. These rules cannot and must not be used as a substitute for careful structural engineering in any actual building. If so used, they could result in excessive structural deflection or outright collapse; or, less seriously, in an uneconomically conservative structural design. The rule-of-thumb values are useful as preliminary assumptions for the designer; but that is the limit of their usefulness.

WOOD FRAME

GETTING STARTED LAYING OUT FOUNDATIONS

When designing a foundation to fit a floor plan, proceed as follows:

1. Simplify the perimeter of the foundation by constructing all possible protruding parts of the floor above as overhanging bays, using cantilevered floor joists.

2. The floor plan can often be adjusted slightly in shape and size, to eliminate small jogs in the foundation layout.

3. Design the floor framing layout at the same time as you design the foundation. Let each adjust as necessary to accommodate the other.

4. Framing lumber comes in standard lengths of 8', 10', 12', 14', and 16'. Plywood subflooring is applied in 4'x8' sheets. Where possible, adjust foundation dimensions to accommodate these materials without waste.

5. Standard formwork is usually made to a 12" module, so whole-foot exterior dimensions are easier to form.

6. Residential foundation walls are usually 8" to 10" thick.

GETTING STARTED LAYING OUT WOOD FRAMING

The layout of framing for a floor, a wall, or a roof of a small wood building is based on a simple set of principles:

1. A set of parallel members two inches in nominal thickness are spaced 16" or 24" apart to frame the surface:

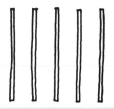

2. Similar members are nailed across the ends to form a single assembly:

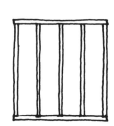

3. Where an opening is required in the surface, members are doubled all around the opening:

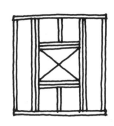

4. Finally the surface is sheathed with boards, plywood, or other sheet materials:

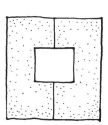

a general procedure for laying out wood framing is as follows:

1. Decide on the best direction for the framing members to run.

2. Lay out the framing members around openings, edges, and other special conditions.

3. Add the ordinary framing members.

There are slight variations on this basic theme which should be kept in mind when laying out the various parts of a building:

FLOORS

1. Decide on a direction of framing which will allow the use of 2×8 or 2×10 joists with only one or two straight lines of interior supporting beams or walls. Keep to a single size of joist throughout, and make the basic layout as simple as possible.

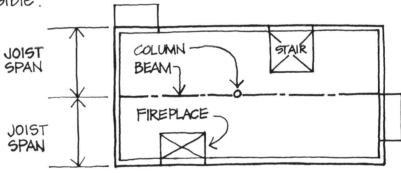

2. Draw in double headers and trimmers around openings for stairs and fireplaces. Use joist hangers for such butt-jointed intersections of framing.

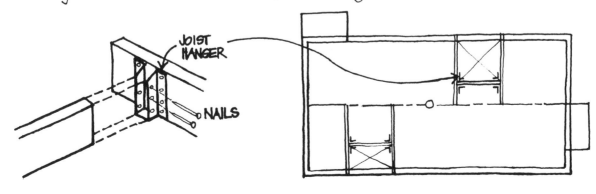

3. Lay out the edges of framing for overhanging bays. Double any joists which support walls. Joists which cantilever for an overhanging bay should not project more than about one-fifth of their maximum allowable span. The interior portion of a cantilevered joist should be at least twice as long as the projecting portion, and preferably, three times as long.

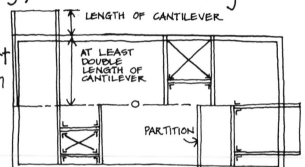

4. Lay out double joists for support of any interior partitions which run parallel to joists.

5. Fill in the framing plan with single joists working faithfully to a 16" module that starts at one edge of the building and runs to the other without interruption. This assures that edges of sheets of plywood subflooring will always occur over joists. Where joists are supported by headers, use sheet metal joist hangers.

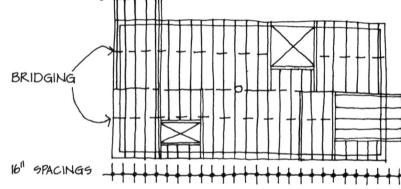

6. If bridging is required, one line should be placed across the midspan of any span over eight feet, and two lines across the third points of any span over sixteen feet.

Some rules-of-thumb spans for ordinary residential floor framing:

2 × 6   spans   8'-0"   maximum
2 × 8   spans   10'-7" maximum
2 × 10   spans   13'-6" maximum
2 × 12   spans   16'-5" maximum

FOUNDATIONS AND FLOOR FRAMING

You've designed a sub-division of houses whose outlines are shown below. Now, draw freehand the foundation plan and floor framing for each, including approximate joist sizes, steel beams, and lines of bridging as required. The subfloor is ⅝" CDX plywood. Assume that the steel beam can span up to 15' between posts.

EXAMPLE:

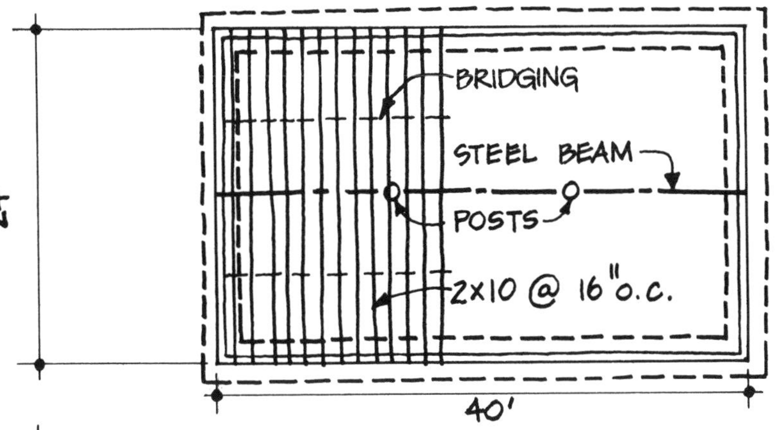

BRIDGING
STEEL BEAM
POSTS
2x10 @ 16"o.c.
24'
40'

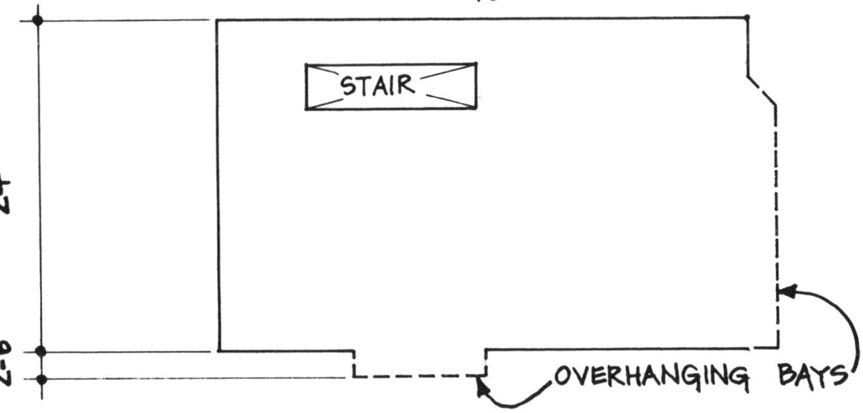

STAIR
24'
2'-6"
OVERHANGING BAYS

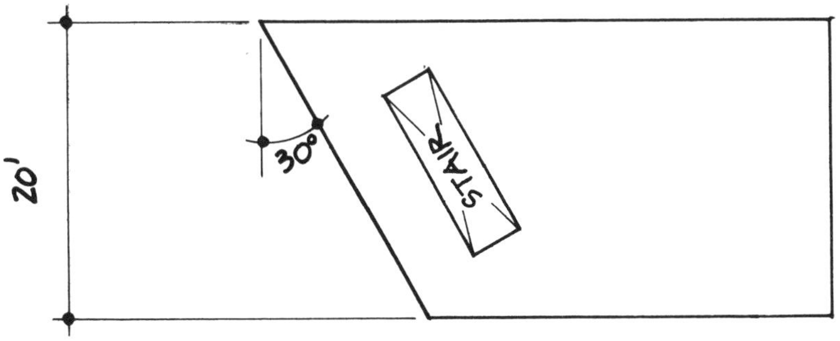

20'
30°
STAIR

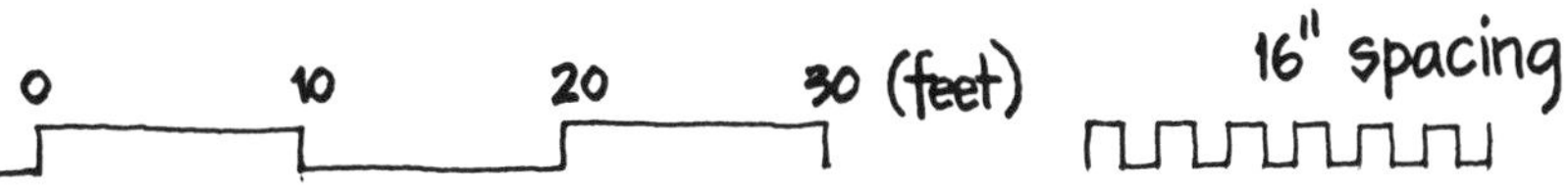

0
10
20
30 (feet)
16" spacing

name ____________

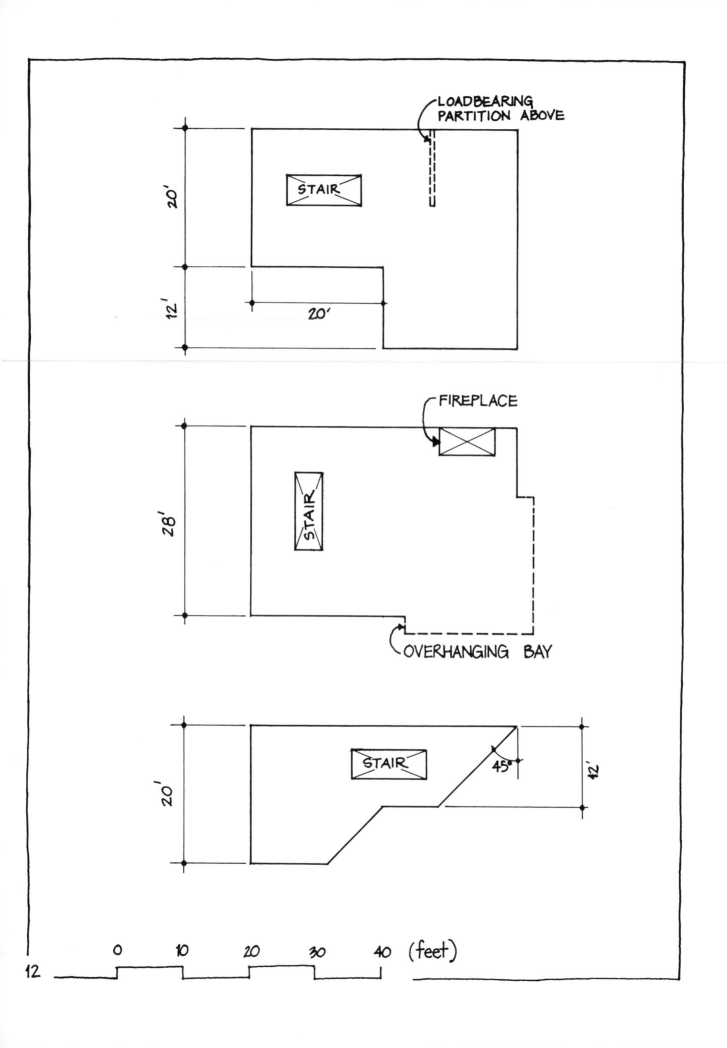

LOADBEARING
PARTITION ABOVE

STAIR

20'

12'

20'

FIREPLACE

STAIR

28'

OVERHANGING BAY

STAIR

20'

45°

42'

0   10   20   30   40   (feet)

12

GETTING STARTED DRAWING CONSTRUCTION DETAILS

Construction details are the language with which you communicate to the craftspeople constructing a building how the building is to be built. They are a key link in a chain of events between the architectural vision and the built reality. Whole volumes have been written on the finer points of the art of detailing. Here are a few hints to get you started:

1. A detail is nearly always a <u>section</u> <u>drawing</u>. The place where the section is cut is usually identified by a line on another drawing, together with an arrow or point showing which way one looks to view the section, and a letter or number to identify the detail drawing.

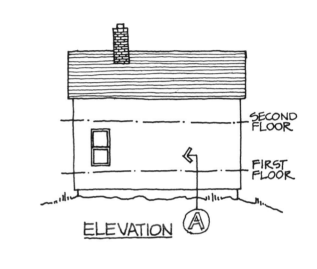

SECOND FLOOR

FIRST FLOOR

<u>ELEVATION</u> (A)

2. In designing a detail, think through and draw the detail in the sequence in which it will be built. Imagine how each construction step takes place and be sure your detail takes into account the problems of the craftspersons doing the work.

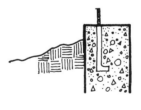

a) draw foundation, earth, and anchor bolt

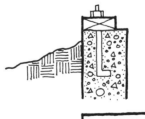

b) draw sill fastened to anchor bolt

c) draw floor framing and subfloor resting on sill, etc.

3. If there are alternative ways of doing something, or if you want to try different materials on the same detail, use cheap tracing paper to try the various alternatives. When you have chosen the best alternative, copy it onto your drawing and go on to the next construction step.

4. Always keep in mind that a building is three-dimensional. Someplace behind the plane of your drawing, your detail will have to join with another detail at a corner. A quick freehand perspective on scratch paper is often useful in resolving corner intersections.

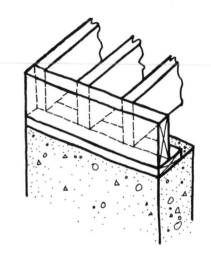

5. When your detail drawing is complete, outline with a heavier line the parts which have been cut by your section. Label the various components. If required, show the letter or number key to the drawing from which the detail is taken.

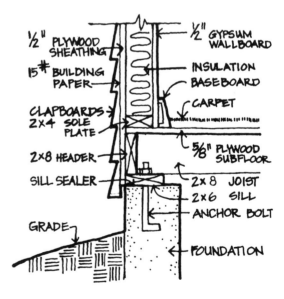

½" PLYWOOD SHEATHING
15# BUILDING PAPER
CLAPBOARDS
2×4 SOLE PLATE
2×8 HEADER
SILL SEALER
GRADE

½" GYPSUM WALLBOARD
INSULATION
BASEBOARD
CARPET
5/8" PLYWOOD SUBFLOOR
2×8 JOIST
2×6 SILL
ANCHOR BOLT
FOUNDATION

DETAIL Ⓐ

GETTING STARTED WITH WALL FRAMING

1. For each window or door opening, a header must be provided, held up by two supporting studs. The same sort of detail should be used for support of any major beam.

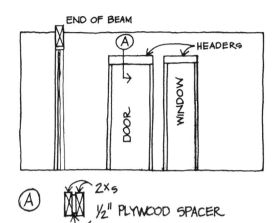

END OF BEAM

A

HEADERS

DOOR

WINDOW

A 2×s
½" PLYWOOD SPACER

2. Add a single horizontal 2×4 sill piece under each window. Add full-length studs to hold each header assembly in place.

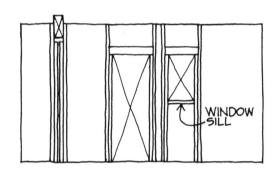

WINDOW SILL

3. Add special assemblies of full-length studs for corner posts and partition intersections.

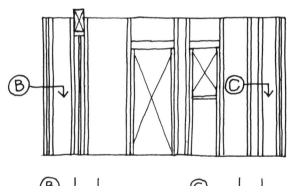

B

C

B   C

4. Fill in the wall with studs, working faithfully to a 16" module that starts at one edge and runs to the other without interruptions. This assures that edges of sheets of wall sheathing will always occur over studs.

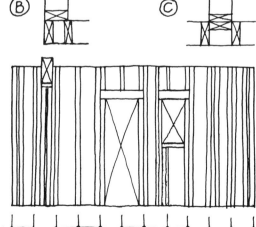

16" modules

5. Add a double 2×4 top plate and a single 2×4 sole plate.

6. If diagonal braces are required, locate them so they run as close to 45° as possible, while still avoiding openings. They should run from the very top of the wall to the very bottom.

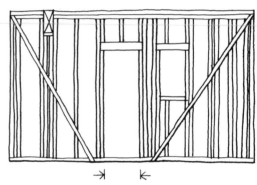

Note: sole plate will be cut out of doorway after wall is in place

2×4 studs 16" o.c. are good for all cases except as follows:

a. The lowest floor of a 3-story building must be framed with 2×6 or 3×4 studs.

b. Walls with a clear height of more than 11'-0" must be framed with 2×6 studs.

WALL FRAMING

1. Diagram freehand the framing of this exterior wall. Assume that 2×4s are used throughout except for double 2×8 headers over windows and doors. Studs are spaced 16" on center. Show in the drawing the sole plate, studs, top plate, corner posts, headers, and supporting studs for headers. Also show detail cross-sections as indicated.

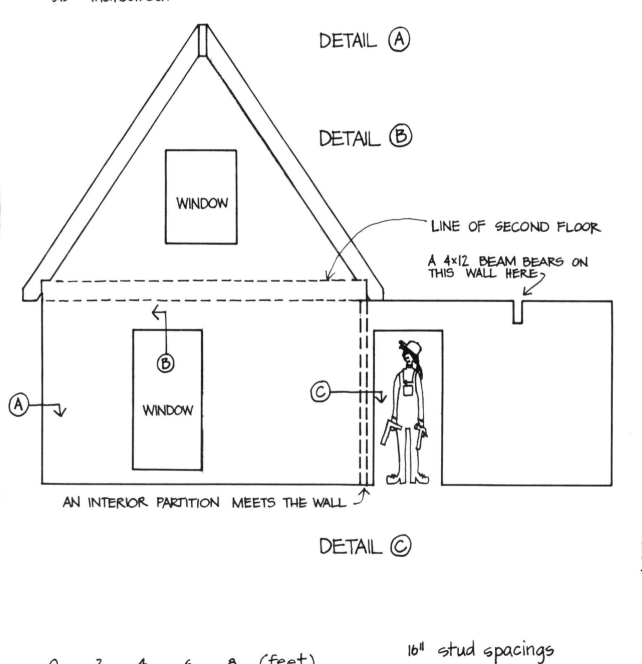

DETAIL Ⓐ

DETAIL Ⓑ

WINDOW

LINE OF SECOND FLOOR

A 4×12 BEAM BEARS ON THIS WALL HERE

Ⓑ

WINDOW

Ⓐ

Ⓒ

AN INTERIOR PARTITION MEETS THE WALL

DETAIL Ⓒ

0   2   4   6   8   (feet)

16" stud spacings

2. Draw and name all framing members in these two cross-section details of a building, including subfloor, wall sheathing, and roof sheathing. Optional: Show interior and exterior finish materials.

A. UNDERLINE EAVE DETAIL

B. UNDERLINE DETAIL AT FOUNDATION

FOUNDATION WALL

GROUND

0 2 4 6 8 10 12 (inches)

GETTING STARTED WORKING WITH PITCHED ROOF CONFIGURATIONS

Roofs are pitched (sloped) because we can waterproof pitched roofs with shingles rather than a waterproof membrane. A minimum pitch for a roof is established by the type of shingles used. Steeper pitches than the minimum are selected for any of several possible reasons:

To mold the roof as closely as possible to the interior space of the building ...

To achieve a desired appearance...

To improve the weathertightness of a roof exposed to severe weather conditions...

Roofs at shallower pitches are somewhat more economical, because they use less material to cover a given building area, and because the roofers can work on the roof without scaffolding.

The sloping underside of a pitched roof presents unique opportunities to the designer which can be maximized by making skillful use of the rising and falling ceilings within the building. Some rooms need taller ceilings than others. Sometimes the sloping ceiling can help focus attention on a particular part of the room, or on a window with a desirable view. Where a ceiling becomes very high, a second floor level can be inserted beneath it, perhaps a balcony or mezzanine within the larger space. As you become more conversant in the vocabulary of pitched roofs, you will be able to make more of these sorts of things happen in your buildings.

The basic building-block of pitched roof configurations is the shed or single-pitched roof:

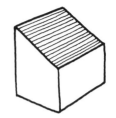

Two sheds together make a gable roof:

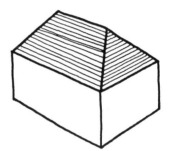

Two intersecting gables make a hip roof:

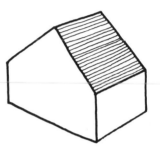

Or a dormer:

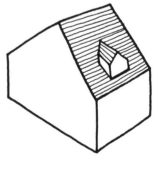

Sheds of different pitches can combine to produce a gambrel roof, or a mansard roof, or a shed dormer:

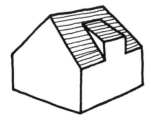

SHED DORMER

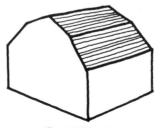

GAMBREL

MANSARD

Pitched roofs can be added together to house almost any collection of interior spaces:

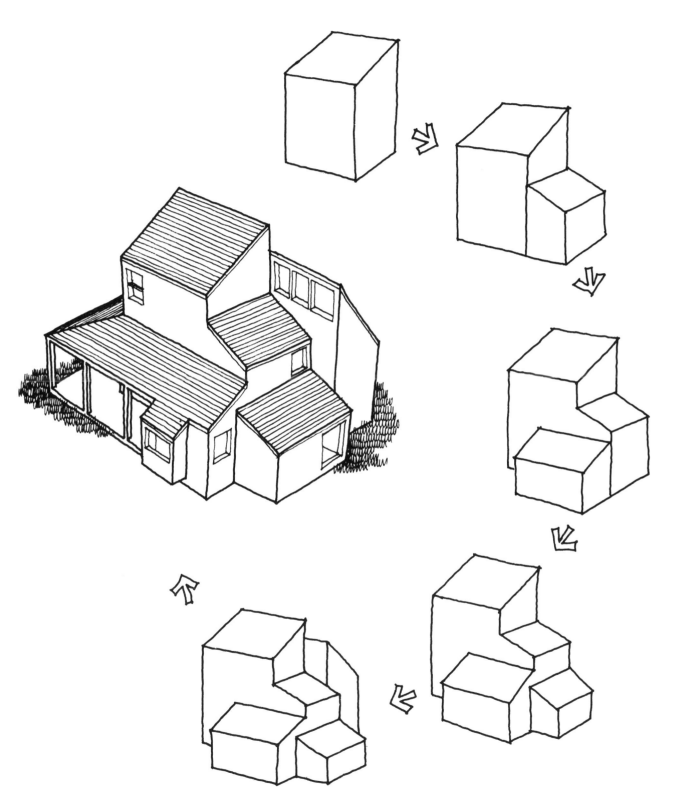

Every day you see buildings about you which are covered with pitched roofs. Observe each one closely, to analyze the reasons for its form. How is the roof configuration affected by the floor plan, and vice versa? Do the interior spaces take advantage of the possibilities offered by the varying roof heights? In what directions do the roof slopes run, and why? Is the window arrangement related to the roof form in any significant way? How was the pitch angle selected? Learn the language of roofs by "listening" to it as you look at the buildings of others — and by "speaking" it, as you design buildings of your own.

ROOF CONFIGURATIONS

1. Sketch at least 12 ways, preferably more, of covering an L-shaped building with one or more roof planes, all at an 8/12 pitch. Indicate changes of roof plane with a single line, and the direction of drainage of each plane with an arrow. Wall planes may be introduced between roof planes. Level valleys are to be avoided. In addition, draw a thumbnail perspective of each scheme.

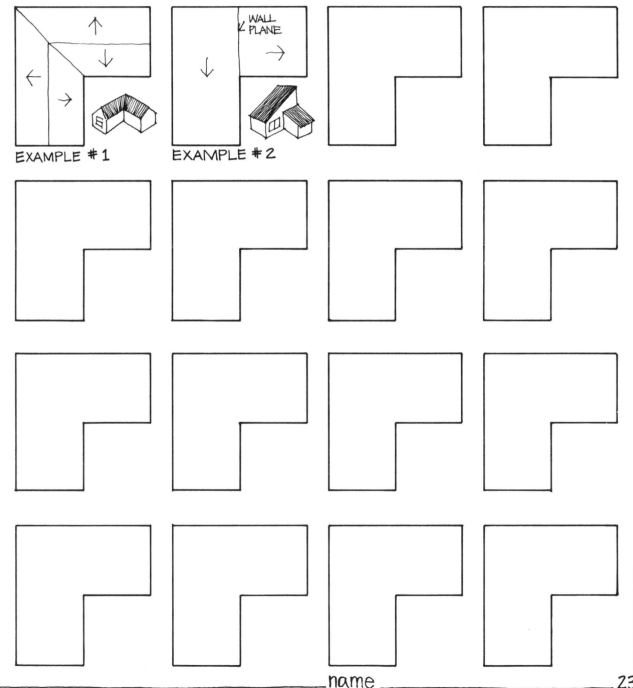

EXAMPLE #1   EXAMPLE #2

2. Now sketch different ways of covering the buildings below with one or more roof planes, all at an 8/12 pitch. In addition, draw a thumbnail sketch of each scheme.

1 story

2 story

2 story throughout

Needs maximum sunlight from south side

2 story   1 story porch

1 story, good view to south-east

2 story

0   8   16   24

N

GETTING STARTED WORKING WITH ROOF PITCHES

Roof pitches are normally expressed in inches of rise (vertical dimension) per twelve inches of run (horizontal dimension). This is done for the convenience of the carpenter laying out the rafters, who uses a framing square to lay out the length of the rafter and the various end cuts.

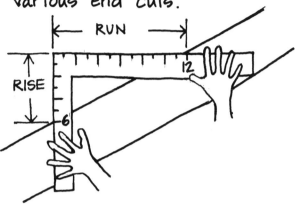

There are two convenient ways to do calculations with roof pitches. The first is to set up a proportion using the given rise and run:

a) Find the height "y" of the roof at a distance of 7'-6" from the edge.

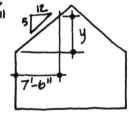

Solution:

$$\frac{5}{12} = \frac{y}{7.5}$$

$$y = \frac{5(7.5)}{12} = \frac{37.5}{12}$$

$$y = 3.125' = \underline{3'-1\frac{1}{2}''}$$

The second, when using a pocket calculator, is to find the tangent of the angle of roof slope:

b) Same example

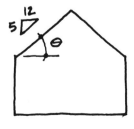

Solution:

$$\tan \theta = \frac{5}{12} = 0.4167$$

$$\theta = 22.62°$$

$$y = 7.5 \tan \theta = 3.125$$

$$y = \underline{3'-1\frac{1}{2}''}$$

25

This second approach is especially useful when you need to know other things about the roof:

c) What is the distance "r" along the surface of the roof in the preceding example which corresponds to a run of 11'-9"?

<u>Solution:</u>

$11'-9" = 11.75'$

$\theta = 22.62°$

$\dfrac{11.75}{r} = \cos\theta$

$r = \dfrac{11.75}{\cos\theta}$

$r = \dfrac{11.75}{.923} = 12.73$

$r = \underline{12'-8\frac{3}{4}"}$

A third way of working with roof pitches is to lay out the pitch accurately to scale, using mechanical drawing instruments, and to measure any required lengths with an architect's scale, thus avoiding using any calculations at all. This is the easiest way to work if you are at a drawing board and have the instruments handy. This procedure is sufficiently accurate for most purposes. Mathematical calculations are better if you are away from a drawing board, or if you need very accurate results. They are especially handy when you are designing a building with freehand sketches, and need a quick check on interior headroom or required roof pitch.

WORKING WITH ROOF PITCHES

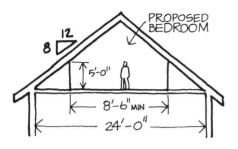

1. A roof starting from the attic floor at a pitch of 8/12 spans an attic 24' wide. The local building code requires that a bedroom be at least 8'-6" wide, and that no part of the bedroom may have a ceiling lower than 5'-0". Can this attic be converted into a bedroom? Show all calculations.

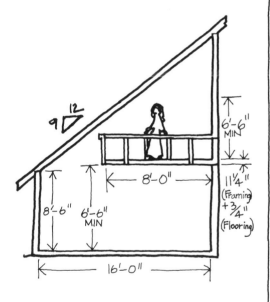

2. A shed roof, starting from the top of the double top plate of the wall framing at a height of 8'-6", rises at a pitch of 9/12 and spans a first floor 16' wide. Is there room to put in an 8' wide mezzanine as a second floor if the local building code requires that no part of the ceiling be lower than 6'-6"? Show all calculations.

3. The staircase at the right has 14 risers of 7.4" and 13 treads of 10." What is the minimum roof pitch which will give a minimum headroom of 6'-6" at the top of the stairs?

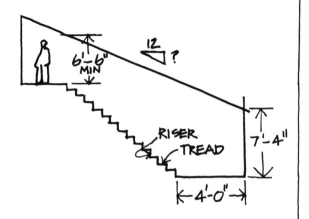

4. An optimum tilt for a flat-plate solar collector for wintertime heat collection is approximately equal to the geographic latitude plus 15°. Express in whole inches of rise per foot of run the optimum roof pitch for a flat-plate collector in St. Paul, Minnesota (latitude 45°).

5. (a quickie!) A 5/12 roof will rise how many feet across a roof surface 22 feet wide as measured on the floor plan?

GETTING STARTED WITH ROOF FRAMING

1. It is almost always advantageous for rafters to run up and down the slope of the roof, rather than across the slope. (This is mainly because rafters which run across the slope tend to sag downward toward the eave.)

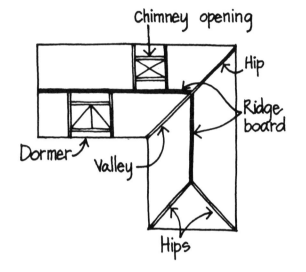

2. Start by laying out the ridge board and the double rafters at the special conditions: chimney openings, dormers, hips and valleys.

3. Lay out the common rafters and jack rafters on a 16" or 24" module, to assure a match with sheets of plywood sheathing.

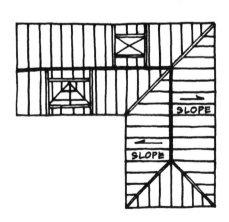

4. Unless supported at ridges and other breaks in pitch by walls or beams, roof types such as gable, gambrel, hip, and mansard, need to be tied securely with ceiling or floor joists to prevent spreading, as shown in the diagrams:

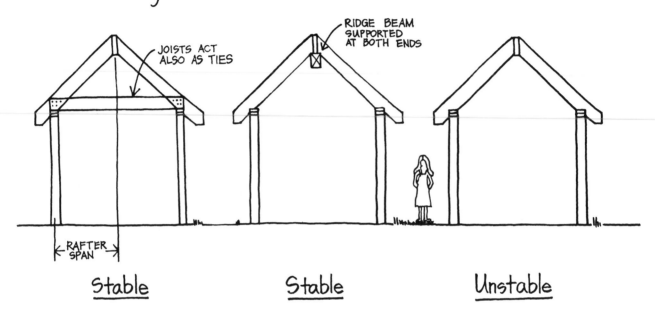

JOISTS ACT ALSO AS TIES

RIDGE BEAM SUPPORTED AT BOTH ENDS

←RAFTER SPAN→

Stable   Stable   Unstable

5. Some rule-of-thumb spans for rafters:
(note: spans are measured from the framing plan, not along the slope of the roof)

2 × 4	16" o.c.	spans	6'-0"
2 × 6	16" o.c.	spans	9'-0"
2 × 8	16" o.c.	spans	12'-0"
2 × 10	16" o.c.	spans	15'-6"

ROOF DESIGN

1. Shown at right is the floor plan of a wood-land cabin. In the space below draw a longitudinal section and a thumbnail perspective for a roof suitable for wood shingles. Be sure to leave plenty of headroom in the loft while not making the area around the stove ridiculously tall. The loft floor is 7'-9" above the main floor. Show the numerical roof pitch and all critical dimensions on the section. Note: The roof may consist of any number of roof planes.

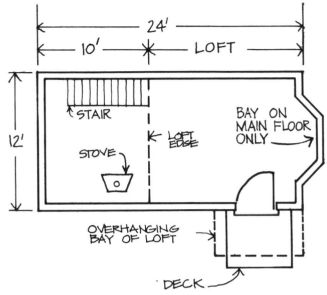

24'

10' * LOFT

STAIR

12'

STOVE

LOFT EDGE

BAY ON MAIN FLOOR ONLY

OVERHANGING BAY OF LOFT

DECK

0 2 4 6 8 10 12 (feet)

2. Show how simple your roof design from the previous page really is: draw a framing plan for it. Use 16" rafter spacing, and give rule-of-thumb rafter sizes.

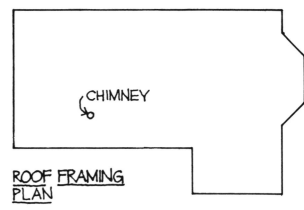

ROOF FRAMING PLAN

3. Show how the rafters are cut to rest on the top of the lowest wall of the cabin. Try two different alternatives, one without an overhang, the other with a 12" overhang.

Ⓐ NO OVERHANG

Ⓑ OVERHANG

4. Draw and label the framing members for this roof plan. Assume 2×6 rafters throughout. Use 24" rafter spacing.

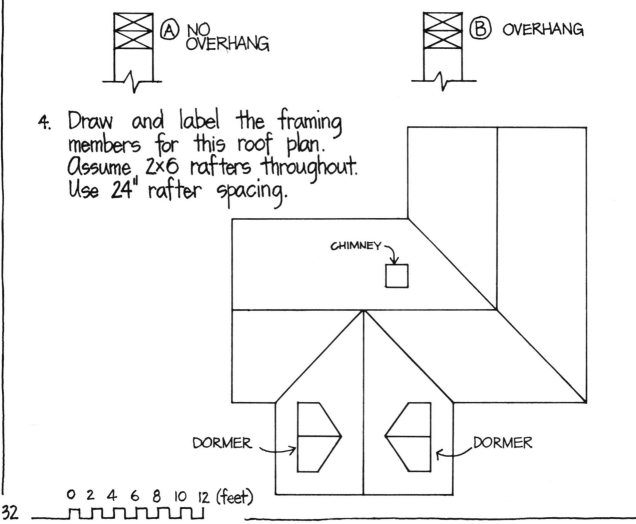

CHIMNEY

DORMER   DORMER

0 2 4 6 8 10 12 (feet)

FIGURING BOARD FOOTAGE OF LUMBER

Lumber is measured and priced in dollars per board foot, and (more commonly) in dollars per thousand board feet. A board foot is a volume of lumber which is nominally one inch thick, twelve inches wide, and twelve inches long. Thus, a 1×12 board ten feet long contains ten board feet of lumber. Similarly, a 2×6 ten feet long contains ten board feet. A general formula for board measure is:

$$\text{Board feet} = \frac{\begin{array}{c}\text{Thickness} \\ \text{in inches}\end{array} \times \begin{array}{c}\text{Width} \\ \text{in inches}\end{array} \times \begin{array}{c}\text{Length} \\ \text{in feet}\end{array}}{12}$$

Notice that <u>nominal</u> lumber dimensions are used, not actual.

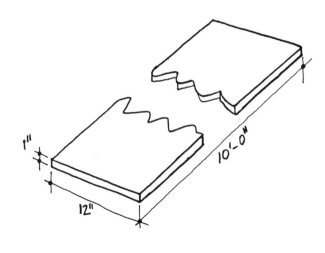

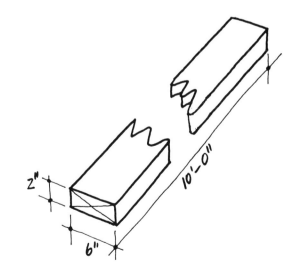

10 BOARD FEET   =   10 BOARD FEET

BOARD FOOTAGE

1. If a 2×4 8' long costs $1.60, how much is that in dollars per thousand board feet? Show calculations.

2. How much will the lumber cost, at $290 per thousand, to frame a wall containing 30 2×4s each 8 feet long? Again, show your work.

3. A certain residential floor can be framed with 39 joists, each 14 feet long. If #2 Hemlock is used at a cost of $284 per thousand board feet, 2×10s must be used. If Douglas Fir is used instead, its greater stiffness allows the use of 2×8s, but at a cost of $342 per thousand. Which is the more economical way to frame the floor? Show calculations.

GETTING STARTED DESIGNING STAIRS

Building code requirements for stairs generally boil down to something like this:

	Minimum Width	Maximum Riser Height	Minimum Tread depth	Minimum Headroom
Residential attic or basement stairs	30"	8"	9"	6'-6"
Main residential stairs	36"	8"	9"	6'-6"
Nonresidential stairs	44"	7¾"	10"	6'-8"

Where a stair turns, a landing must be provided. The width of the landing should not be less than the width of the stair.

Treads and risers must be geometrically proportioned for comfort and safety. The procedure for doing this is as follows:

1. Calculate the overall rise of the stair in inches, floor-to-floor.

2. Divide the overall rise by 7, and round off to determine the number of risers in the stair.

3. Divide the overall rise by the number of risers to determine the riser height to two decimal places.

Example:

Floor-to-floor height $= 9'-7\frac{3}{8}''$

$9'-7\frac{3}{8}'' = 115\frac{3}{8}''$

$\frac{115\frac{3}{8}''}{7} = 16.48$, use 16 risers

$\frac{115\frac{1}{4}''}{16} = 7.21''$

Riser height $= 7.21''$

4. Substitute the riser height, R, into the formula: $2R + T = 25$

and solve for T, the depth of the tread. The tread depth can be rounded off slightly if desired.

$2(7.21") + T = 25$

$T = 25 - 14.42$
$T = 10.58"$,

use 10.6".
Tread depth = <u>10.6"</u>

5. Summarize your calculations. (There are always one fewer treads than risers in a stair.) Check your answers against the code requirements.

<u>16 risers @ 7.21"</u>

<u>15 treads @ 10.6"</u>

6. If a steeper or shallower stair is desired, add or subtract a riser and recalculate. The most comfortable riser heights for most interior stairs lie in the range of 6½" to 7½".

STAIR DESIGN

1. Using the stair formula 2R + T = 25, calculate appropriate numbers and dimensions of treads and risers for the following stairs. Show all calculations.

   a) ATTIC STAIR, total rise 104", minimize total run.

   b) MAIN STAIR, in a residence, total rise 8'- 11½" total run not critical.

   c) EXIT STAIR in a high school, total rise 12'-8"

   d) ENTRANCE STEPS to a courthouse, total rise 4'-9".

2. The loft floor of a summer cottage is 8'-2¼" above the main floor. Compute the numbers and dimensions of treads and risers for the steepest permissible stair. Show all calculations.

3.

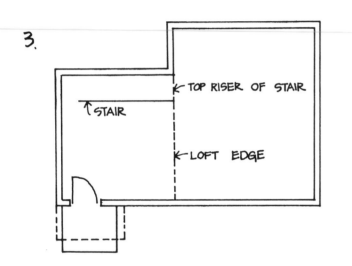

TOP RISER OF STAIR

STAIR

LOFT EDGE

0 2 4 6 8 10 12 (feet)

This is the floor plan of the cottage. Assuming the stair is 30" wide, and remembering that any landing or turning space must be equal in length to the width of the stair, will the stair fit in the designated space on the floor plan above as a single flight of steps? YES _____ or NO _____
Draw on the plan how this stair can be fitted in.

4. For the exit stair you calculated
in exercise 1c of the previous page,
assume a stair width of 44".
Draw in the space to the right
how this stair can be laid out
to be entered from a 36" wide
door at the same location on each
floor. What are the overall inside dimensions of the stair enclosure?

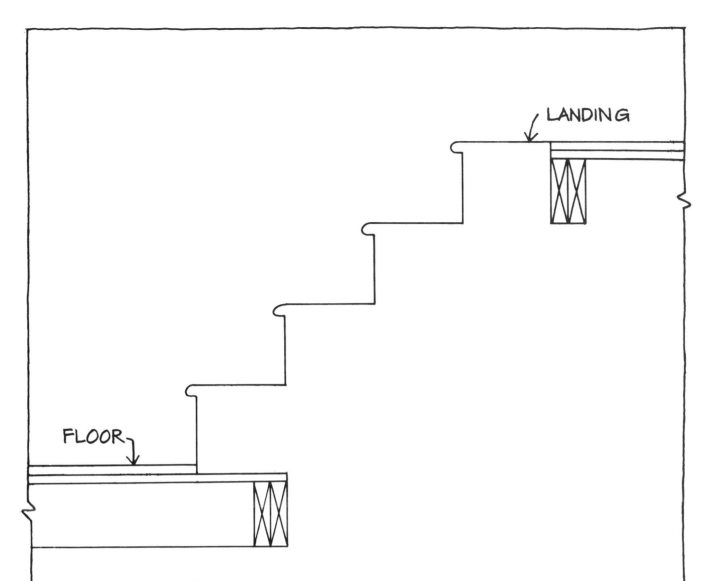

LANDING

FLOOR

5. An outline for the cross-section of a staircase is shown above. Draw in the RISERS, TREADS, and CARRIAGE or STRINGER.

6. You're in a hurry to finish some first rough design drawings of a building, and you want to indicate some stairways in cross-section by simply drawing in sloping lines to represent the line of nosings. Which of these easily-drawn angles approximates most closely the slope of a well-proportioned stair?

15°___   30°___   45°___   60°___

0 2 4 6 8 10 12   (inches)

7. A neighborhood social center which you are designing needs a major stair leading from the middle of the ground floor lobby, to the large room above which serves for public meetings, exercise classes, weekend dances, and various large social functions. The neighborhood committee wants something broad, straight, and somewhat ceremonial. The floor-to-floor height is 11'-3½". Proportion this stair, and draw a perspective of how you would like it to look. Draw a construction detail of a portion of the stair, indicating materials to be used.

GETTING STARTED WITH INSULATION

The overall coefficient of heat transmission, U, is a measure of how rapidly a roof, wall, or floor acts as a heat conductor. So, a wall with a high U-value does not insulate as well as a wall with a lower U-value. In numbers, U is expressed as:

the rate of heat loss in Btu per hour
through one square foot of surface
with a 1°F temperature difference
between the inside and outside air.
(Btu / hr / ft.² / °F)

U-values cannot be calculated directly. Instead, we must use the reciprocal expression of thermal conductance which is thermal resistance:

$$R = \frac{1}{U}$$

The use of R-values, or thermal resistances, is convenient because R-values for all the materials in a roof, wall, or floor can be added directly to give an overall resistance, R_T. We can then calculate the overall values of U as:

$$U = \frac{1}{R_T}$$

Notice that a well-insulated wall has a higher R-value than a poorly-insulated wall, and a lower U-value.

Here are some common building materials with their corresponding R-values:

MATERIAL	R-VALUE
Outside air film, 15 mph wind	0.17
Wood siding, lapped	0.81
½" CDX Exterior plywood sheathing	0.63
15# Asphalt building paper	0.06
Wood (framing): fir, pine, softwoods	0.91 (per inch)
3½" Airspace	1.01
½" Gypsum wallboard	0.45
3½" Mineral wool batt	10.90 (3.12 per inch of thickness)
1" Rigid polystyrene foam	4.10 (per inch)
Inside air film (insulating value of air layer adhering to wall surface)	0.68

Window glass has the following U-values:

Single pane, $U = 1.13$
Double pane, $U = 0.61$
Triple pane, $U = 0.41$
Glass block
$(8" \times 8" \times 4")$, $U = 0.56$

Here is a typical calculation for an uninsulated wall:

	R-value
Inside air	0.68
½" Gypsum wallboard	0.45
3½" airspace	1.01
½" CDX Exterior plywd.	0.63
15# Building paper	0.06
Lapped wood siding	0.81
Outside air	0.17
R_T	3.81

$U = \dfrac{1}{R_T} = \dfrac{1}{3.81}$

$U = \underline{0.26}$

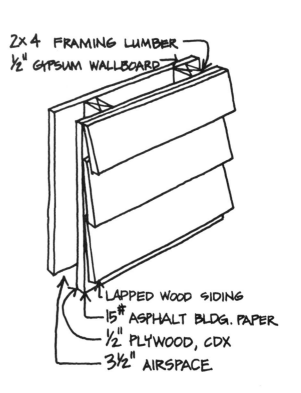

2×4 FRAMING LUMBER
½" GYPSUM WALLBOARD
LAPPED WOOD SIDING
15# ASPHALT BLDG. PAPER
½" PLYWOOD, CDX
3½" AIRSPACE

CALCULATING INSULATION VALUES

For purposes of comparison with the uninsulated stud wall in the example, calculate R and U values for each of the following examples:

1. "Well-insulated" wall: Add 3½" mineral wool batt

    R____   U____

2. "Well-insulated" wall plus 1" polystyrene foam sheathing in place of plywood

    R____   U____

3. Wall with 2×6 studs, ½" plywood sheathing, and 5½" mineral wool batt

    R____   U____

4. Double-pane "insulating" glass

    R____   U____

5. What is the ratio of the rate of heat loss through double pane "insulating" glass to the rate of heat loss through a "well-insulated" wall?

6. Which of the walls on the other side of this page would qualify as the R-19 wall required in many solar-heated and electrically-heated residences?

DESIGN EXERCISE IN WOOD

Two young professionals are very interested in your designing a prototypical building for their wine, bread, and cheese shops WITH THE GRAIN. The structures are to be built on a half-dozen sites in New England country villages. You have agreed on the following design criteria:

1. For both thermal efficiency and ease of construction, platform-frame construction is to be used.

2. Each food shop is to be a single story with a floor area of 750 ft², the ceiling at the rafter line, and café seating for 20 persons in an upper loft.

3. All materials for finishes, inside and out, are to be consistent with the village setting of the food shops; simplicity and minimal maintenance are desirable.

a. LIST A SET OF MATERIALS which might be appropriate for such shops, specifying species, grade, and/or method of sawing, as necessary.

1. FRAMING LUMBER :
2. SUB-FLOOR :
3. ROOF and WALL SHEATHING :
4. ROOFING :
5. BUILDING PAPER :
6. SIDING :
7. INSULATION :
8. VAPOR BARRIER :
9. FASCIAS, CORNER BOARDS, WINDOW TRIM :
10. INTERIOR CEILING FINISHES :
11. INTERIOR WALL FINISH :
12. FLOORING :
13. STAIR TREAD MATERIAL :

_____ name _____ 45

14. STAIR RISER MATERIAL:
15. FRONT DOOR:
16. FRONT PORCH (shop entry):
17. TYPE OF WINDOW which will allow outdoor views without air infiltration on windy winter days:

18. TYPE OF WINDOW which, if accidentally left open, will still keep out most rain and snow:

19. TYPE OF WINDOW which will help catch passing summer breezes:

20. HEATING SYSTEM:

B. DRAW FREEHAND

1. A small diagrammatic floor and foundation plan of a simple natural food shop that is consistent with your points of agreement with your clients:

2. A small perspective to go with the floor and foundation plan:

3. A small roof-framing diagram:

4. A complete rake or eave detail
   using the materials you have
   specified :

   guidelines for thickness
   of 2x4 stud

5. A complete detail of the
   intersection of the upper
   eating loft with an outside
   wall, again using materials
   you have specified:

6. A complete detail of the
   sill of the window you
   have specified under
   #17, as installed in wall :

   0   3   6   9   12 (inches)

MASONRY

GETTING STARTED DESIGNING BRICKWORK

Although a particular brick bond may be used for its decorative effect, the original and primary purpose of bonding is to tie a brick wall together into a single structural unit. For a single wythe of brick, such as a brick facing over a wood-frame wall, 'running bond' is the logical choice. For a wall of two or more wythes, common bond is economical and lends itself well to walls with a concrete-block backup. If brick is used instead of block as a backup, the stronger and more complex bonds, such as English and Flemish, may be used. These are much richer visually than running or common bonds, but they involve large numbers of headers, and of cut bricks at corners, and are therefore difficult and more expensive to lay.

The selection of a jointing method is usually governed by weather resistance for exterior brickwork, and by visual considerations for interior walls. Weathered joints and concave joints are most resistant to weather damage. Weathered and raked joints create a shadow line at each course. Other jointing methods create various kinds of visual effects: a beaded joint calls attention to the surface pattern of the mortar joints; a stripped joint produces a wall in which the mortar is not seen; an extruded joint gives a casual, rustic appearance.

MASONRY BONDS

In the spaces below, draw elevations and corresponding sections of masonry bonds as indicated, using bricks the size of the scale brick given at the bottom of the page. The sections are of a nominal 8" wall.

←— outside corner of two intersecting walls

English Bond, weather joint

Flemish Bond, raked joint

Common or American Bond, concave joint

0 3 6 9 12 (inches)

BRICK:

name

Any other bond of your choice

Coursed Rubble stone

Random ashlar stone

BRICK:

0   3   6   9   12 (inches)

GETTING STARTED WITH LINTELS AND ARCHES

The designer of any masonry building is faced with the problem of how to support masonry over openings in the walls. Three basic solutions to this problem have been developed through the ages:

1. The corbel is the least sophisticated of the three, and produces a shape of opening which can be hard to fill with a window or door. Each course should project not more than ⅓ the length of a brick or stone.

2. The lintel is simply a beam which carries the load of the masonry above and transfers it to the wall on either side. Originally of wood or stone, most lintels are now made of steel, of reinforced concrete, or of reinforced masonry.

Wood or Stone Lintel

Reinforced Concrete Lintel

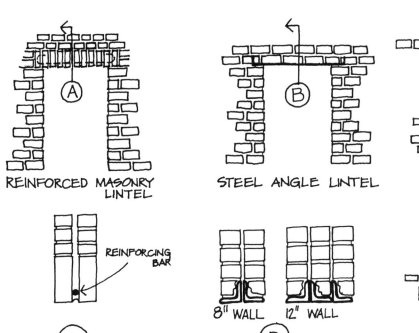

REINFORCED MASONRY LINTEL

STEEL ANGLE LINTEL

REINFORCING BAR

Ⓐ

8" WALL   12" WALL

Ⓑ

3. The arch is the most sophisticated of masonry spanning devices, and comes in many forms. Arches can be built of specially-shaped stones or bricks called voussoirs, or they can be built of unshaped units, in which case they are called rough arches. Rough arches are much easier and cheaper to build and are therefore more common. Many shapes of arch have been developed. All of them exert a lateral thrust. This thrust is usually buttressed adequately by the masonry of the surrounding wall, provided the span is not very great, nor the opening too close to the end of the wall. An arch is built over a simple wooden formwork known as centering.

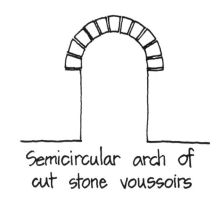

Semicircular arch of cut stone voussoirs

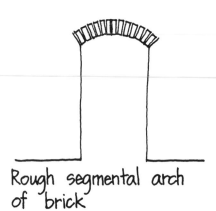

Rough segmental arch of brick

Tudor arch

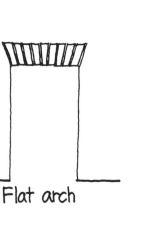

Rough Stone arch

Flat arch

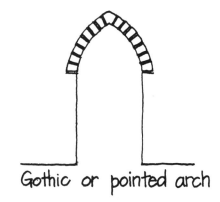

Gothic or pointed arch

LINTELS AND ARCHES

Draw in both elevation and section an appropriate design for each of the following openings:

1. Doorway 36" wide and about 7' high in an 8" Flemish bond garden wall which is 9' high overall

ELEVATION   SECTION

2. Double-hung aluminum window 3'-0" wide in 8" wall, common bond

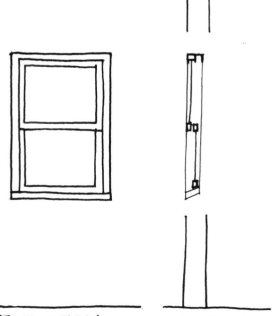

ELEVATION   SECTION

0 1 2 3 4 (feet)

name

3. 48"-wide opening, 36" high in a fieldstone fireplace

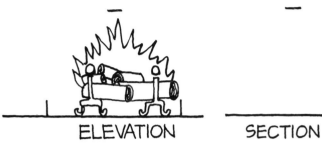

ELEVATION   SECTION

4. Branch bank entrance, 12' wide in a 12" wall composed of 4" of coursed ashlar granite over an 8" concrete block back-up.

ELEVATION   SECTION

0   1   2   3   4 (feet)

GETTING STARTED WITH MASONRY DIMENSIONING

It is usually easiest to calculate masonry dimensions by figuring the dimension of one masonry unit plus one mortar joint, and making this the module for the construction. For example:

Length of brick   8¼"
Mortar joint   + ⅜"
Basic Module   8⅝"

(Note: This is an example. Bricks come in many different sizes. Base your dimensioning for an actual job on the exact bricks you will use.)

If a wall is built by laying seven of these particular bricks end-to-end, it will look like this in plan:

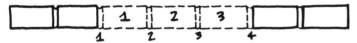

You can see that this wall contains seven bricks, but only <u>six</u> mortar joints. Therefore its outside-to-outside length can be figured as:

Length of wall = 7(8⅝") − ⅜" = <u>60"</u> or <u>5'-0"</u>

If three of the bricks are removed from this wall to make an opening, the inside-to-inside width of the opening will be three bricks plus <u>four</u> mortar joints:

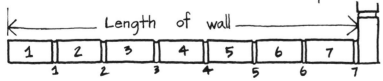

Width of opening = 3(8⅝") + ⅜" = <u>26¼"</u> or <u>2'-2¼"</u>

And if a second wall is added at right angles to the first, the length of the wall becomes seven bricks plus seven mortar joints:

Therefore, these general rules for masonry dimensioning:
1. Outside-to-outside dimension = n modules − 1 mortar joint
2. Inside-to-inside dimension   = n modules + 1 mortar joint
3. Outside-to-inside dimension   = n modules exactly

These same general rules apply to <u>vertical</u> dimensions of masonry as well as to <u>horizontal</u> dimensions. A masonry wall always starts with a mortar joint at the bottom, and generally finishes at the top without a mortar joint. If the foundation upon which the wall sits is very uneven, the bottom mortar joint may be made thicker to produce a level first course.

Modular brick courses utilize bricks approximately 2¼" high with ⅜" mortar joints, so three courses with three mortar joints measure 8" in height. Each course is thus 2⅔" in height, but overall height dimensions are frequently rounded to the nearest ⅛".

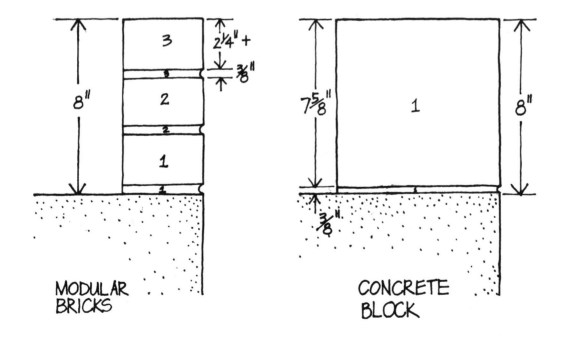

MODULAR
BRICKS

CONCRETE
BLOCK

MASONRY DIMENSIONING

1. The small retail store building whose plan is drawn below is to be built of standard 8x8x16 (nominal) concrete blocks on a concrete slab floor. In order to start the working drawings, you must first work out the exact plan dimensions of the masonry. Fill-in the dimensions accurate to the nearest ⅛", in such a way that only full blocks and half-blocks need be used, without any cutting of blocks. Check your work by seeing if each chain of dimensions adds up to the corresponding overall dimension.

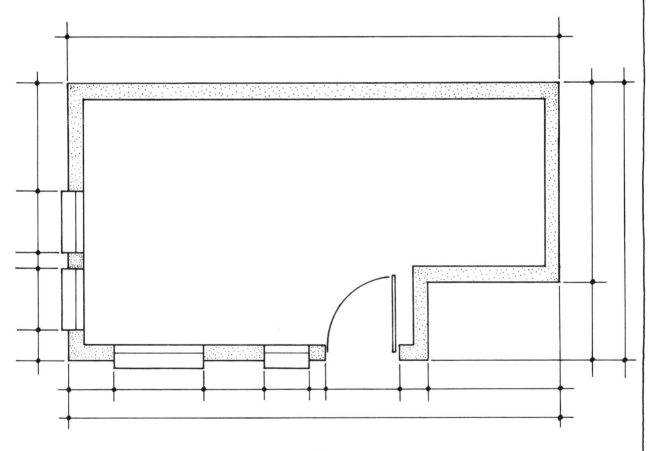

2. How many block courses will be needed to support ceiling joists at a height of about 9½', and what will be the exact height? _____
_____

3. If the building were to be built of brick instead of block, figure the number of courses and the exact height of the wall to achieve a nominal 9½' ceiling height:

NUMBER OF COURSES   HEIGHT

a) Modular brick
(3 courses + 3 mortar joints = 8")

_____   _____

b) Jumbo brick
(2¾" high with ⅜" mortar joints)

_____   _____

c) Utility brick
(3⅝" high with ½" mortar joints)

_____   _____

d) Arizona adobe brick
(4" x 12" x 18" with ½" joints)

_____   _____

GETTING STARTED DESIGNING FIREPLACES

Fireplace design is an art and not a science, and is based on what has worked in the past and what hasn't. A fireplace that will throw a reasonable amount of heat and a minimum amount of smoke into the room will result from the following design procedure:

1. Select a width, W, somewhere between 30" and 60."

2. Make the height of the opening, H, ⅔W to ¾ W. The opening may be arched n-stead of flat.

3. The depth, D, to the fire-box should be ½ H to ⅔ H. A shallower fireplace will throw more heat.

4. The cheeks should slope at an angle between 2/12 and 5/12. 5/12 is preferable.

5. The back of the fireplace should be vertical for a height of H/3, then curve forward to meet the damper.

6. The damper should be set 8" above the top of the fireplace opening.

7. The damper should extend the full width of the fireplace. A damper is a large iron valve which can narrow or close the throat of the fireplace. Before installation it looks so: The flap is controlled by an operating handle or screw.

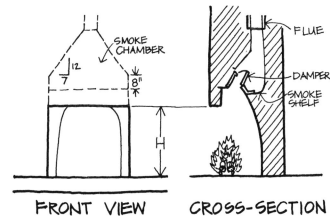

FRONT VIEW   CROSS-SECTION

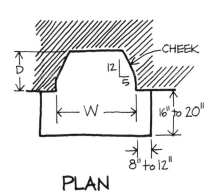

PLAN

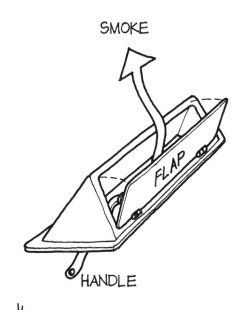

8. Behind the damper, a curving smoke shelf at least 4" wide must be provided to divert cold drafts which may come down the chimney.

9. The front and sides of the smoke chamber should converge on the flue at slopes of 7" in each 12" of height.

10. The inside cross-sectional area of the chimney flue should be 1/10 WH.

11. The chimney should be as tall as possible. It must extend at least 3' above any roof surface within 10 feet. If the chimney is taller than 30 feet above the hearth, the flue area can be reduced to 1/12 WH.

12. A masonry or concrete hearth must extend 8" to each side for a small fireplace and 12" for a large one. Its depth should be 16" to 20".

13. A steel angle lintel, concrete lintel, or masonry arch should support the masonry over the fireplace opening.

14. The fireplace should be constructed of 8" of solid masonry with a firebrick lining, and must be supported by its own incombustible foundation.

The above procedure is based on Albert G.H. Dietz, <u>Dwelling House Construction</u>, M.I.T. Press, 1974. Local building codes should be consulted for possible variations from this procedure.

FIREPLACE DESIGN

The opening of the brick fireplace on the back of this page is 40" wide as the plan indicates.

1. Indicate the appropriate DIMENSIONS for the hearth and firebox areas:

   a = _____   Minimum depth of hearth

   b = _____   Width of hearth extension on each side of opening

   c = _____   Depth of firebox

   d = _____   Angle of slope of cheeks as ratio$\left(\frac{x}{12}\right)$

   e = _____   Height of opening

   f = _____   Size of flue in square inches (in^2) of free area

2. Lay out a BRICK PATTERN for the hearth. A brick drawn to scale can be found at the bottom of page.

3. On both elevation and section, draw in the back of the firebox, the lintel, the damper, the smoke shelf, the smoke chamber, and the flue tile.

4. On the elevation, design a BRICK PATTERN for the fireplace facing, using the scale brick and mortar joint as shown on opposite page.

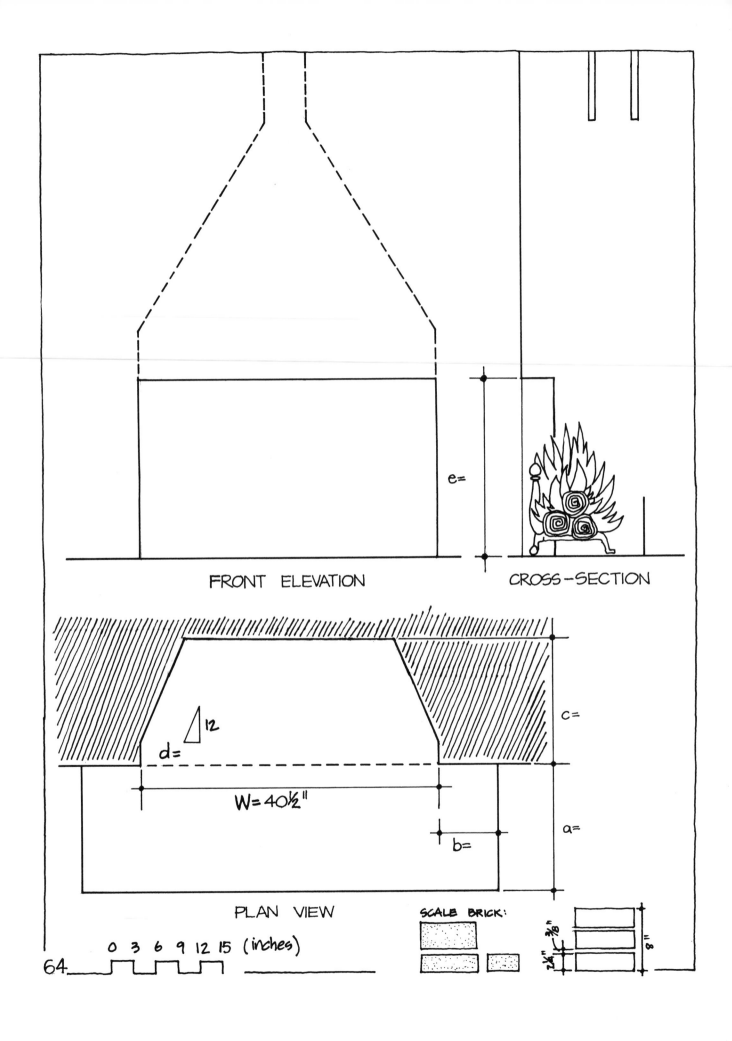

FRONT ELEVATION

CROSS-SECTION

e=

c=

d=

△12

W= 40½"

b=

a=

PLAN VIEW

SCALE BRICK:

0 3 6 9 12 15 (inches)

2¼"   ⅜"   8"

64

MASONRY BEARING WALL DETAILS

In the spaces to the right draw complete cross-section details:

line of outer face of wall ⟶

1. Edge of flat roof, factory building, 8" precast concrete planks, 8" concrete block walls, no overhang, minimal fascia, ½" gypsum wallboard over 1" furring and insulation on walls, 2" foam insulation on roof.

2. Edge of intermediate floor, 3-story commercial building, mill construction, 12" solid brick exterior wall.

0   6   12   18   24   (inches)

3. Edge of warehouse roof, cavity wall, brick facing, insulated cavity, 8" block back-up, open-web steel joists, 2" corrugated steel roof deck, 3" foam roof insulation, 30" parapet with stone coping.

0   6   12   18   24   (inches)

DESIGN EXERCISE IN MASONRY

A family of five in San Diego, California, have asked you to design a simple weekend retreat for them in the dry hills of Baja California. They would like to use burned brick for long-term durability. A family of highly-skilled Mexican masons will do the work. A simple two-room plan is envisioned, with one generous room for cooking, eating, and socializing; and another, with full bath, for sleeping. An outdoor shaded patio is also desired. The roof should be well-insulated against solar heat gain.

a. LIST A SET OF MATERIALS which might be appropriate for such a retreat:

1. FOUNDATION:
2. FLOOR:
3. WALLS:
4. ROOF STRUCTURE:
5. ROOF INSULATION:
6. ROOFING:
7. CEILING FINISH:
8. FRONT DOOR:
9. PATIO PAVING:

B. DRAW FREEHAND: (in the spaces to the right)

1. A small diagrammatic floor and foundation plan of a simple two-room retreat:

(exercise continued on following pages) name _____ 67

2. A small, exterior perspective to go with the foundation and floor plan:

3. A small interior perspective, showing the atmosphere created by the structure and finishes you have selected:

4. A roof framing plan:

5. A detail showing roof construction:

6. A detail showing intersection of floor and foundation construction:

7. A plan and perspective
   of the outdoor patio,
   with its brick paving:

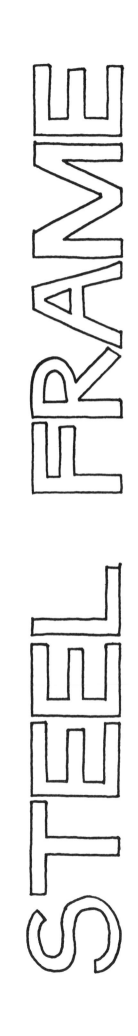

STEEL FRAME

GETTING STARTED LAYING OUT STEEL FRAMING

Steel framing is not so standardized as wood platform framing. Steel wide-flange beam and column sections are produced in a very wide variety of depths and weights, from a W4×13 (4" deep, 13 lbs. per foot of length), to a W36×300, including special column shapes up to a W14×730. Floor and roof decks supported by steel frames can be of many different materials and products with widely varying spanning capabilities. Steel-frame buildings are individually engineered from the ground up, without the use of conventionalized rules-of-thumb such as 16" joist spacing and 2×4 studs. The detailed design of a steel building frame is usually done by a structural engineer who works with the architect. The architect must therefore be conversant in the vocabulary of steel construction, and must be capable of designing feasible steel framing layouts, in order to become competent as a member of the design team for steel-frame buildings.

Assume in preliminary design work that steel columns will be wide-flange sections which are square in proportion, ranging from approximately 6"×6" for a story or two, through 8"×8", 10"×10", and 12"×12", up to 14×14" for very tall buildings. Remember that column size will change in a tall building, becoming larger from top to bottom. Start your layout of a steel framing plan by locating columns for support around elevator shafts, stairways, and other special conditions. Show beams connecting these columns in both directions, and insert beams between elevators to carry the elevator tracks. The orientation of the columns (I or H) is probably not critical, but be consistent throughout the plan. For beam sizes, use a rule-of-thumb depth of $D = \frac{Span}{20}$, rounding off to the nearest 2" up to an 18" depth, and the nearest 3" for depths from 21" to 36". Exact depths, weights, and connection details must be worked out later by means of structural calculations, but this formula will give a fair idea of probable beam depth. (Beam widths are usually about one-half to one-third of their depths.)

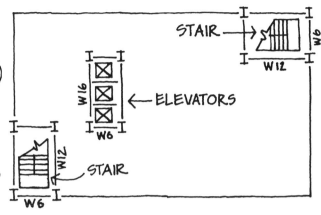

For the remainder of the framing layout, you must decide on an approximately bay size and shape. Bay size depends on many things: What system of decking will you use, and how far can it span? How frequently are you willing to have columns piercing through the interior space? How long a beam or girder span is feasible? (Usually spans are kept in the range of 24' to 36'.) Is the building plan on a modular grid which should be respected in the placement of columns? Form a design hypothesis about the general size and orientation of bays which might fit the building, and use cheap tracing paper over the floor plan to attempt a first freehand framing plan based on your hypothesis. Then adjust the column spacings to fit the floor plan, or adjust the floor plan to fit the column spacings, or form a new hypothesis if necessary, pushing and pulling and trying things out until something works simply and smoothly. In most buildings, bays need not be the same throughout a floor, but in general, a clean, orthogonal layout of framing will be easier and more economical than one which has many ir- regularities and anomalies.

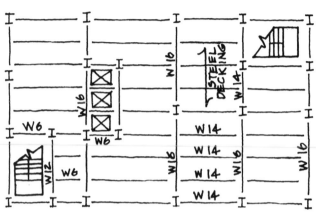

Most steel frames, in order to eliminate as many columns as possible, use both beams and girders. The beams are spaced to carry the floor deck at its maximum allowable span, while the girders carry the beam loads to the columns. Both beams and girders are wide-flange sections.

If the rule-of-thumb formula on the preceding page indicates a girder size that is smaller than the beam size, increase the girder to one size deeper than the beam

BEAMS

GIRDER →

STEEL FRAMING LAYOUT

You are designing a 10-to-15-story regional office building in downtown Omaha, Nebraska, for Associated Mutual Casualty and Life Corporation. Three possible plan arrangements for a typical floor of the building are shown below and following. Draw a feasible framing plan over each of the floor plans, and give approximate depths for the typical beams and girders. Assume that you will use a 1½" deep corrugated steel deck which can span 8'-0" maximum between supports, and W8 columns which are approximately 8" × 8" in cross-section.

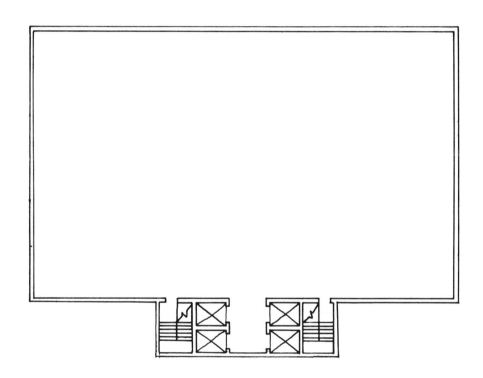

0   10   20   30   40   50   60   70   80   (feet)

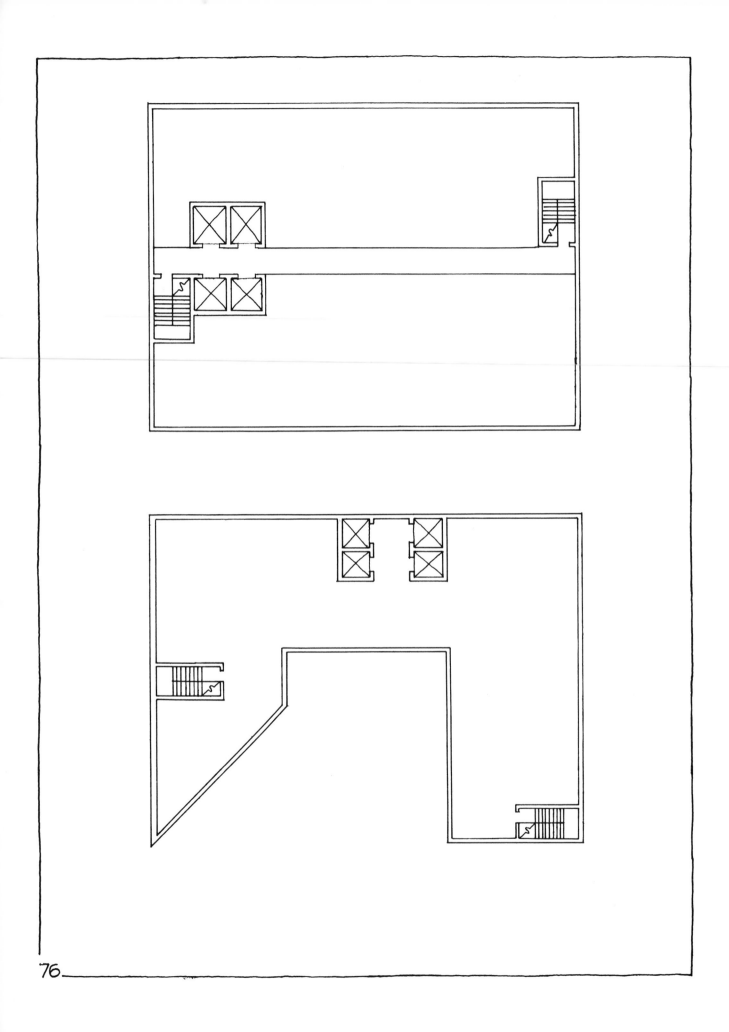

GETTING STARTED DETAILING STEEL CONNECTIONS

Structural steel connections are designed on the basis of the loads they must transmit from one member to another, a subject which is beyond the scope of this book. Independently of exact structural calculations, however, you should become familiar with the more common methods of steel joinery, both bolted and welded. The following exercise will start you in this direction.

Framed connections are used for most purposes, such as beam-to-girder, beam-to-column-flange, and girder-to-column-flange. For connections into column webs, seated connections provide easier accessibility to the bolts for the steel erector.

Beam-to-girder connections should be coped, as shown at the top of the accompanying table of wide-flange shapes, whenever steel decking is used, to provide a level base for the decking. (See page 81)

The top angle in a seated connection serves mainly to keep the beam from twisting, and can be of almost any convenient size.

In any bolted connection, the beam should be cut shorter than the space it is to fill by 1" to 1½", thus providing a setback of ½" to ¾" at each end to allow for easy placement of the beam.

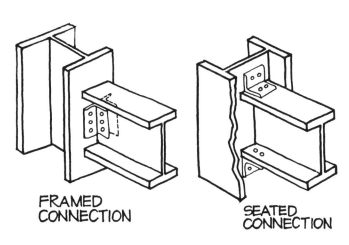

FRAMED
CONNECTION

SEATED
CONNECTION

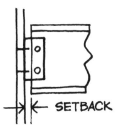

← SETBACK

SOME TYPICAL FRAMED CONNECTIONS

Rows of Bolts	Applicability	Angle Size*	t of angle		
			3/4" bolts	7/8" bolts	1" bolts
2	W12, 10, 8	∠4×3½×5½	5/16	3/8	7/16
3	W18, 16, 14, 12	∠4×3½×8½	5/16	3/8	7/16
4	W24, 21, 18, 16	∠4×3½×11½	5/16	3/8	7/16
5	W30, 27, 24, 21, 18	∠4×3½×14½	5/16	3/8	7/16

* First two figures are dimensions of angle section as shown in drawing; last figure is cut length of angles.

SOME TYPICAL SEATED CONNECTIONS

Type	∠	t
A, D	4 × 3	3/8 – 5/8
	4 × 3½	3/8 – 5/8
	4 × 4	3/8 – 3/4
B, E	6 × 4	3/8 – 7/8
	7 × 4	3/8 – 7/8
	8 × 4	1/2 – 1
C, F	8 × 4	1/2 – 1
	9 × 4	1/2 – 1

Source: American Institute of Steel Construction

STEEL CONNECTIONS

Select any exterior column from any framing plan you have drawn in the previous exercise, and draw details as specified:

1. Shown at lower left is an elevation of a W10×49 column, with a line indicating the level of the bottom of the corrugated steel floor deck. Using the "Dimensions for Detailing" table at the end of this chapter, add to this drawing the beam(s) and girder(s) which join the column, using the wide-flange section which most closely approximates the rule-of-thumb depth which you have calculated. Assume that 7/8" bolts will be used, and use the largest connecting angles which will fit. Be sure to show the setback for each member.

← W 10 × 49

Bottom of Steel Deck

₵ Center line of girder

0 2 4 6 8 10 12 (inches)

2. Design and draw an adjacent beam-girder connection from your same framing plan, centering the cross-section of the girder over the center line at the lower right on the other side of this page.

3. Draw a W10×39 column resting on top of the W10×49 shown on the previous page. Design and draw their connection.

4. In the space below, draw a typical foundation connection of a W10×49 column to a concrete pile cap.

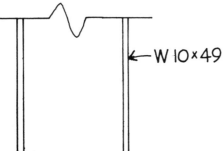

←— W10×49

5. If each column section is two stories high, and the floor-to-floor height is 13 feet, how much does a section of W10×49 weigh? Show calculations.

6. How much will this column section cost if the total installed cost of structural steel is $925 per ton? Show calculations.

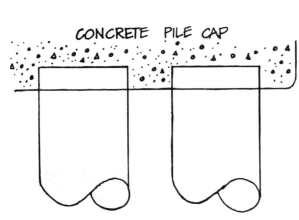

CONCRETE PILE CAP

0 2 4 6 8 10 12 (inches)

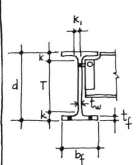

SOME TYPICAL WIDE-FLANGE SHAPES — DIMENSIONS FOR DETAILING

(Source: American Institute of Steel Construction)

Designation	Depth d	Flange Width b_f	Flange Thickness t_f	Web Thickness t_w	$t_w/2$	Distance T	Distance k	Distance k_1
	in.	in.	in.	in.	in.	in.	in.	in.
BEAMS								
W 18×60	18¼	7½	11/16	7/16	¼	15½	1⅜	13/16
W 16×40	16	7	½	5/16	3/16	13⅝	1 3/16	13/16
W 14×34	14	6¾	7/16	5/16	3/16	12	1	⅝
W 12×30	12⅜	6½	7/16	¼	⅛	10½	15/16	½
W 10×26	10⅜	5¾	7/16	¼	⅛	8⅝	⅞	½
W 8×18	8⅛	5¼	5/16	¼	⅛	6⅝	¾	7/16
W 6×12	6	4	¼	¼	⅛	4¾	⅝	⅜
COLUMNS								
W 10×112	11⅜	10¾	1¼	¾	⅜	7⅝	1⅞	15/16
W 10×49	10	10	9/16	5/16	3/16	7⅝	1 3/16	11/16
W 10×39	9⅞	8	½	5/16	3/16	7⅝	1⅛	11/16
W 8×48	8½	8⅛	11/16	⅜	3/16	6⅛	1 3/16	⅝
W 8×35	8⅛	8	½	5/16	3/16	6⅛	1	9/16
W 6×25	6⅜	6⅛	7/16	5/16	3/16	4¾	13/16	7/16

81

CONCRETE FRAME

GETTING STARTED SELECTING CONCRETE FRAMING SYSTEMS

In selecting a concrete framing system for a given building, first decide if the system should be <u>precast</u> or <u>cast-in-place</u>. Precast spanning elements are usually prestressed, which means that they are very slender and efficient, and can span considerable distances. They eliminate the need for most on-site formwork. Because they are brought to the site fully cured, construction can proceed rapidly, without waiting for structural concrete to cure. On the other hand, precast systems are incapable of two-way action and are usually incapable of structural continuity. They are more difficult to adapt to nonrectilinear buildings.

<u>Cast-in-place</u> systems are more time-consuming to erect, but can be adapted to any shape of building, are structurally continuous, are capable of two-way action, and can often be post-tensioned to further increase their structural efficiency. If a cast-in-place system is to be used, a two-way system will be more economical, but the building must be arranged in bays that are square, or within 30% of square. If floor loadings are above 100 psf, a two-way system should be used, or a one-way solid slab.

The chart on the following page will help you to make an initial selection of a concrete framing system.

SELECTING A CONCRETE FRAMING SYSTEM

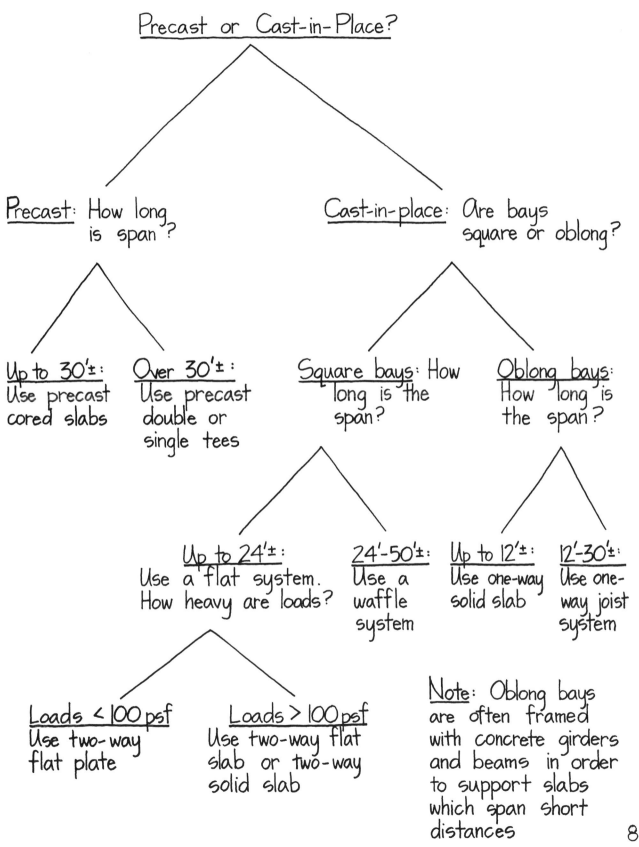

Precast or Cast-in-Place?

Precast: How long is span?

Cast-in-place: Are bays square or oblong?

Up to 30'±: Use precast cored slabs

Over 30'±: Use precast double or single tees

Square bays: How long is the span?

Oblong bays: How long is the span?

Up to 24'±: Use a flat system. How heavy are loads?

24'-50'±: Use a waffle system

Up to 12'±: Use one-way solid slab

12'-30'±: Use one-way joist system

Loads < 100 psf Use two-way flat plate

Loads > 100 psf Use two-way flat slab or two-way solid slab

Note: Oblong bays are often framed with concrete girders and beams in order to support slabs which span short distances

85

SOME RULES-OF-THUMB FOR CONCRETE FRAMING

BEAMS and GIRDERS

Overall depth $\cong \dfrac{span}{15}$

Width $\cong \dfrac{depth}{2}$

> Cast-in-place concrete beams and slabs should be structurally continuous, and should be cantilevered approximately $\dfrac{span}{3}$ at edges, where feasible.

COLUMNS

Cross-sectional area, in² $\cong \dfrac{load}{1000}$, or $\dfrac{gross\ ft.^3\ of\ building\ supported}{50}$

Columns can be round or square. Minimum column dimension is 8".

ONE-WAY SLABS

Overall depth of one-way solid slab $\cong \dfrac{span}{20}$

Overall depth of one-way concrete joist slab $\cong \dfrac{span}{20} + 2\frac{1}{2}"$

    Standard form depths: 8", 10", 12", 14", 16", 20"

    Standard form widths: 20", 30"

    Joist widths can vary 5"-9"

TWO-WAY SLABS

Overall depth of two-way flat plate or flat slab $\cong \dfrac{span}{30}$

Overall depth of two-way waffle slab $\cong \dfrac{span}{30} + 2\frac{1}{2}"$

Module	Joist width	Pan depths
24"	5"	8, 10, 12, 14"
36"	6"	8, 10, 12, 14, 16, 20"
48"	7"	14, 16, 18, 20, 22, 24"
60"	8"	14, 16, 18, 20, 22, 24"

PRECAST

Depth of cored slabs $\cong \dfrac{span}{40}$, standard depths 6", 8", 10"

    standard widths 2', 4'

Depth of tees and double tees $\cong \dfrac{span}{24}$, standard depths: Tees 12"-28"

    Double Tees 10"-24"

SELECTING CONCRETE FRAMING SYSTEMS

For each of the following buildings, name a suitable concrete framing system, and sketch a framing plan for a typical floor bay, giving approximate sizes of all members.

1. Warehouse for a paper company, bays 20' x 22'-4".

2. Rental office building, structural system to be left exposed as finished ceiling, bays 19'-8" square, moveable partition system must be able to meet ceiling at any point.

3. Center-corridor apartment building, 4 stories tall, tight construction schedule, parallel masonry bearing walls along corridor and exterior walls.

4. School, 3 stories, column spacing 21' x 30'.

5. Parking garage, 50' span between lines of parallel supporting beams.

6. Second deck of seats in a professional sports stadium.

7. Metal-casting plant, bays 18'×28'

8. High-rise open-plan office building, bays 38' × 39'-7½".

DESIGN EXERCISE IN REINFORCED CONCRETE

Your firm is hard at work designing a new classroom building for the Northwest Institute of Technology in eastern Oregon. You have already decided that the building should be four stories tall, sixty feet wide, and 120 feet long. A central corridor ten feet wide on each floor will serve the class-rooms and seminar rooms on either side. The structure is to be of concrete, and will be left exposed to the maximum feasible extent both inside and outside the building.

1. In the space below, lay out a framing plan for a typical floor of the building. Use the scale given, and indicate clearly the concrete framing system used, and the approximate thicknesses and other detailed dimensions of its various components.

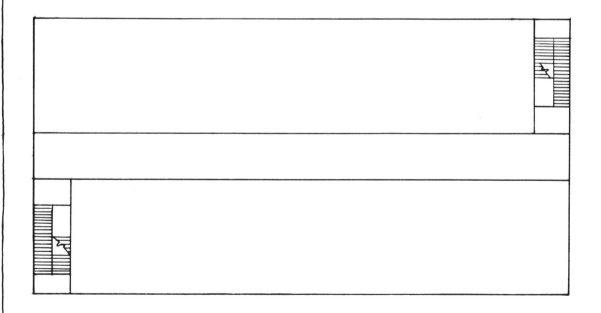

0 5 10 15 20 25 30 (feet)

2. Assuming that a floor-to-ceiling height of 10'-6" is appropriate, draw a cross-section through the entire building to the same scale.

3. Draw either an interior or exterior perspective to show how the concrete framing looks as a part of the finished building.

CONCRETE REINFORCING

Draw a typical reinforcing layout for the concrete frame shown below. (The thicknesses of the components are exaggerated to make your task a little easier.)

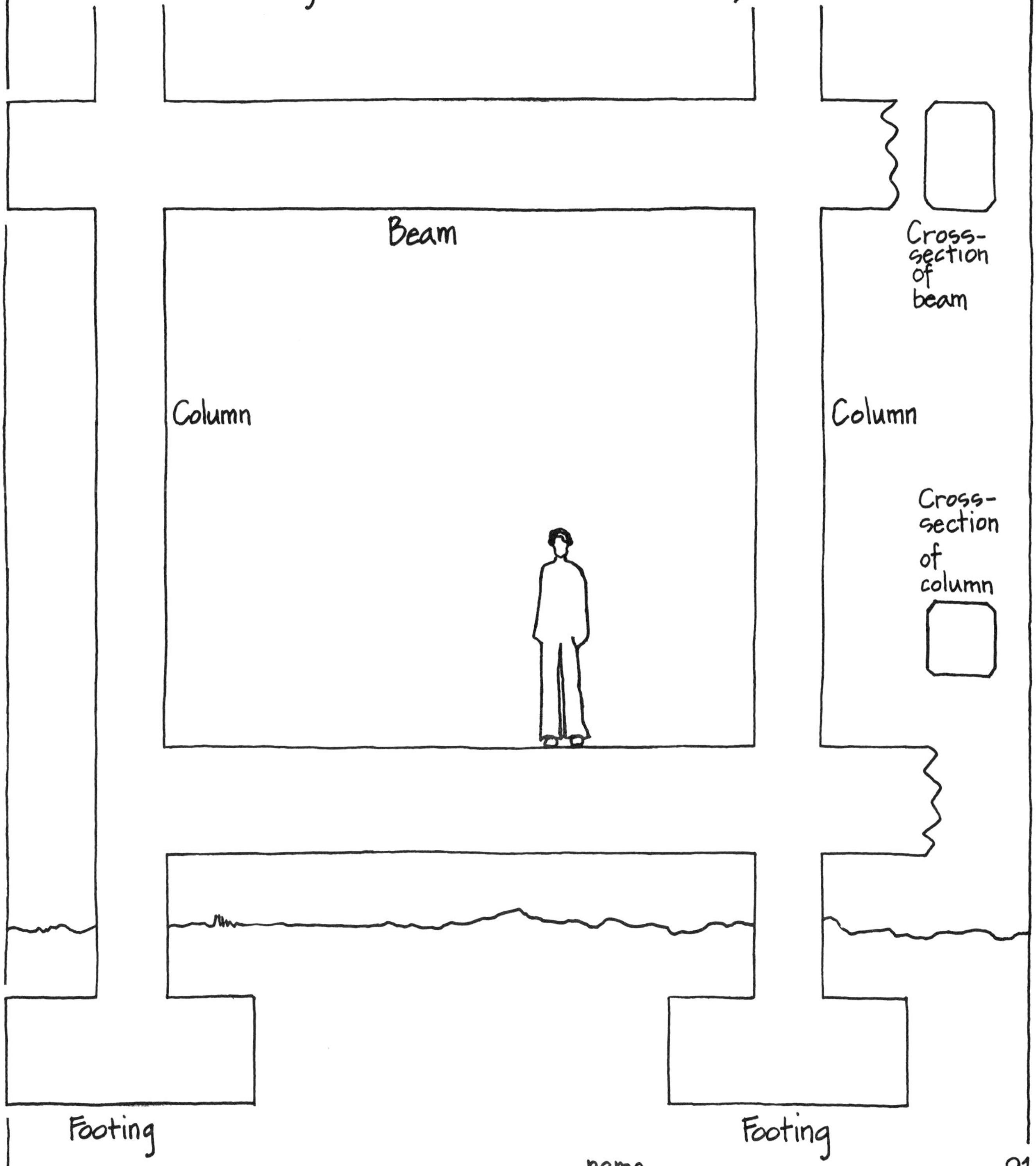

Beam

Cross-section of beam

Column

Column

Cross-section of column

Footing

Footing

LARGER BUILDINGS IN GENERAL

HEIGHT LIMITATIONS IN STORIES AND FEET ABOVE GRADE AND AREA LIMITATIONS IN SQUARE FEET PER FLOOR PER STORY OF BUILDINGS FACING ON ONE STREET OR PUBLIC SPACE NOT LESS THAN 30 FEET WIDE

TYPE OF CONSTRUCTION

USE GROUP		TYPE 1 — Fireproof		TYPE 2 — Noncombustible			TYPE 3 — Exterior Masonry Walls			TYPE 4 — Wood Frame	
				Protected Metal		Unprotected Metal	Heavy Timber (mill)	Ordinary Joisted Protected	Ordinary Joisted Unprotected	Protected	Unprotected
		1A	1B	2A	2B	2C	3A	3B	3C	4A	4B
MERCANTILE		UNLIM	UNLIM	6 ST 75' 22,800	4 ST 50' 15,000	2 ST 30' 9,600	4 ST 50' 14,400	3 ST 40' 13,200	2 ST 30' 9,600	2 ST 30' 10,200	1 ST 20' 4,800
INDUSTRIAL		UNLIM	UNLIM	6 ST 75' 22,800	4 ST 50' 15,000	2 ST 30' 9,600	4 ST 50' 14,400	3 ST 40' 13,200	2 ST 30' 9,600	2 ST 30' 10,200	1 ST 20' 4,800
BUSINESS		UNLIM	UNLIM	7 ST 85' 34,200	5 ST 65' 22,500	3 ST 40' 14,400	5 ST 65' 21,600	4 ST 50' 19,800	3 ST 40' 14,400	3 ST 40' 15,300	2 ST 30' 7,200
ASSEMBLY: THEATERS WITH STAGE AND SCENERY		UNLIM	6 ST 75' 14,400	4 ST 50' 11,400	2 ST 30' 7,500	1 ST 30' 4,800	2 ST 30' 7,200	2 ST 30' 6,600	1 ST 20' 4,800	1 ST 20' 5,100	NOT PERMITTED
THEATERS WITHOUT STAGE (MOVIES)		UNLIM	UNLIM	5 ST 65' 19,950	3 ST 40' 13,125	2 ST 30' 8,400	3 ST 40' 12,600	3 ST 40' 11,550	2 ST 30' 8,400	1 ST 20' 8,925	1 ST 20' 4,200
ASSEMBLY: LECTURE HALLS TERMINALS RESTAURANTS		UNLIM	UNLIM	5 ST 65' 19,950	3 ST 40' 13,125	2 ST 30' 8,400	3 ST 40' 12,600	3 ST 40' 11,550	2 ST 30' 8,400	1 ST 20' 8,925	1 ST 20' 4,200
ASSEMBLY: CHURCHES, SCHOOLS		UNLIM	UNLIM	5 ST 65' 34,200	3 ST 40' 22,500	2 ST 30' 14,400	3 ST 40' 21,600	3 ST 40' 19,800	2 ST 30' 14,400	1 ST 20' 15,300	1 ST 20' 7,200
INSTITUTIONAL: INCAPACITATED		UNLIM	8 ST 90' 21,600	4 ST 50' 17,100	2 ST 30' 11,250	1 ST 20' 7,200	2 ST 30' 10,800	2 ST 30' 9,900	1 ST 20' 7,200	1 ST 20' 7,650	NOT PERMITTED
RESIDENTIAL: HOTELS		UNLIM	UNLIM	9 ST 100' 22,800	4 ST 50' 15,000	3 ST 40' 9,600	4 ST 50' 14,400	4 ST 50' 13,200	3 ST 40' 9,600	3 ST 40' 10,200	2 ST 35' 4,800
RESIDENTIAL: MULTI-FAMILY		UNLIM	UNLIM	9 ST 100' 22,800	4 ST 50' 15,000	3 ST 40' 9,600	4 ST 50' 14,400	4 ST 50' 13,200	3 ST 40' 9,600	3 ST 40' 10,200	2 ST 35' 4,800
RESIDENTIAL: 1,2 FAMILY		UNLIM	UNLIM	4 ST 50' 22,800	4 ST 50' 15,000	3 ST 40' 9,600	4 ST 50' 14,400	4 ST 50' 13,200	3 ST 40' 9,600	3 ST 40' 10,200	2 ST 35' 4,800

STRUCTURAL ELEMENT	TYPE 1 FIREPROOF		TYPE 2 NONCOMBUSTIBLE			TYPE 3 EXTERIOR MASONRY WALLS			TYPE 4 WOOD FRAME	
			PROTECTED METAL		UNPROTECTED METAL	HEAVY TIMBER (MILL)	ORDINARY JOISTED			
							PROTECTED	UNPROTECTED	PROTECTED	UNPROTECTED
	1A	1B	2A	2B	2C	3A	3B	3C	4A	4B
EXTERIOR WALLS On street lot lines or with fire separation of 30' or more from interior lot lines or any building — Bearing	4	3	2	3/4	0	2	2	2	3/4	0
Non-Bearing	0	0	0	0	0	0	0	0	3/4	0
On interior lot lines or less than 6' therefrom, or from any building — Bearing	4	3	2	1½	3/4	2	2	2	3/4	3/4
Non-Bearing	2	2	1½	3/4	3/4	2	2	2	3/4	3/4
Interior bearing walls	4	3	2	3/4	0	2	3/4	0	3/4	0
Fire Enclosure of Exitways, Elevator Hoistways, Exitway Hallways and Stairways	2	2	2	2	2	2	2	2	3/4	3/4
Exitway Access Hallways and Vertical Separation of Tenant Spaces	3/4	3/4	3/4	3/4	0	3/4	3/4	0	3/4	0
Other Non-Bearing Partitions	0	0	0	0	0	0	0	0	0	0
Columns, Girders, Trusses (other than roof trusses) and Framing — Supporting one Floor or Roof	3	2	1½	3/4	0	COLUMNS 8×8 MIN., BEAMS 6×10 MIN., FLOOR DECKING 3″ MIN.	3/4	0	3/4	0
Supporting more than One floor	4	3	2	3/4	0		3/4	0	3/4	0
Floor Construction including Beams	3	2	1½	3/4	0		3/4	0	3/4	0
Roof Construction including Beams 15' or Less in Height	2	1½	3/4	3/4	0		3/4	0	3/4	0
Roof Trusses and Framing including Arches and Roof Deck — More than 15' but less than 20' in height to lowest member	3/4	3/4	3/4	0	0		0	0	3/4	0
20' or more in height to lowest member	0	0	0	0	0		0	0	0	0

GETTING STARTED SELECTING CONSTRUCTION SYSTEMS

The system of construction which you may use in a building is primarily determined by two factors, the <u>fire zone</u> in which the building will be located within a city, and the <u>building code requirements</u> for the building. The building code requirements are based on the use to which the building will be put, and the height and floor area of the building

The charts on the preceding two pages are excerpted and condensed from a typical building code. Enter the first chart by reading down the "Use Group" column until you find an appropriate designation for the building you are working on. Go across the page to the right and read <u>backwards</u> across the row, moving from right to left, until you find numbers for the building height and area per floor which equal or exceed the figures for your building. Reading up the column from these figures, you will find the lowest classification of construction which is permissible. You may select a higher classification if you wish, but you should keep in mind that lower classifications are usually cheaper.

Having identified the type of construction you will use, you may enter the second chart to determine the necessary fire resistances of the various elements of the building. The two pages which follow list some examples of building elements with varying degrees of fire resistance. (These examples are selected from much longer lists published by organizations such as the Fire Underwriters and the Gypsum Association.) You will notice that Type 1 construction may be either of protected steel or concrete framing.

SOME TYPICAL FIRE RESISTANCES

COLUMNS

Resistance	CONCRETE Thickness of cover	STEEL protected with: Plaster on metal lath, thickness:	Gypsum block or board, thickness:	Spray-on fireproofing	
				Exact thickness depends on brand used	
4 HR	1½"	1¾"	3"	2" to 3"	
3 HR	1½"	1⅜"	2" on steel studs	1" to 2"	
2 HR	1½"	1"	2" tight to column	½" to 1"	
1 HR	1"	⅝"	1" tight to column	½" ±	

BEAMS, GIRDERS, FLOORS

Resistance	CONCRETE Thickness of cover	WOOD JOISTS ceiling construction	STEEL BEAM spray-on fireproofing	STEEL JOISTS & BEAMS with concrete floor: Metal lath and plaster ceiling, thickness	Gypsum board ceiling, thickness	
			Exact thickness depends on brand used			
3 HR	1½" beams 1" slabs	not allowed	1" to 3"	⅝"	⅝"	
2 HR	1½" beams 1" slabs	not allowed	1" to 2"	⅝"	½"	
¾ HR	1" beams ¾ slabs	½" gypsum board or plaster	1" ±	⅝"	½"	

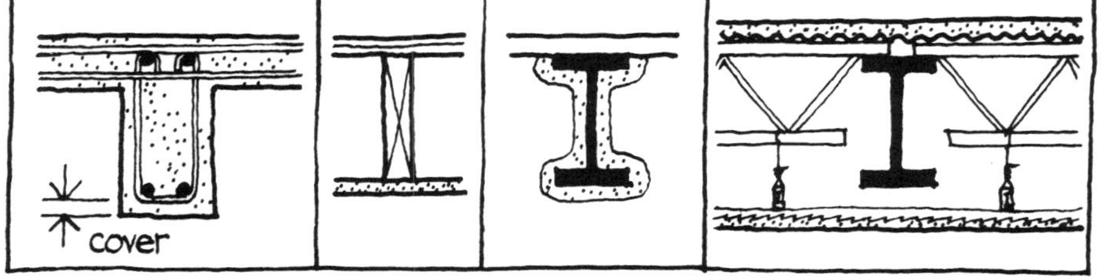

SOME TYPICAL FIRE RESISTANCES

INTERIOR WALLS AND PARTITIONS

	2×4 wood studs	Sheet metal studs, gypsum board both sides	Wire studs, metal lath and plaster both sides	Gypsum Block Wall	Concrete Wall	Stone Wall
4 HR	N.A.	N.A.	N.A.	4" block, ½" plaster both sides	7½"	12"
3 HR	N.A.	N.A.	N.A.	3" block, ½" plaster both sides	6½"	12"
2 HR	2 layers 5/8" gypsum board each side	3⅝" studs 2 layers 5/8" each side	2½" studs 3/4" plaster		5½"	12"
1 HR	5/8" gypsum board or 3/4" plaster each side	3⅝" studs 5/8" each side			4"	8"
¾ HR	½" gypsum board each side	3⅝" studs ½" each side				

N.A. = not applicable

98

SELECTING TYPES OF CONSTRUCTION

Use information from the preceding tables to answer the following questions:

1. An old chocolate factory of heavy-timber construction with brick exterior bearing walls is being considered for conversion to a summer-stock theater in a small South Carolina town. The factory is two stories high, and each floor is 40'×70'. Will this conversion be permitted? _____ What fire resistance rating must you use in new partitions which you add to this building? _____

2. What is the maximum total floor area which can be built in a clothing store of protected platform-frame construction? _____ Can you use exposed heavy-timber beams in this store? _____

3. Name three alternative construction systems suitable for an electronics plant 4 stories high, 12,000 ft.² per floor: _____ _____ _____
   Which system is the most economical? _____

4. What is the maximum permissible height for a reinforced-concrete office tower of Type 1A construction? _____ Which structural element requires the greater amount of fire protection, a beam or a column? Why? _____
   _____
   Can you use protected wood-stud partitions in this building? _____

5. How high can you build a wood-frame house with exposed timbers? _____

6. You have decided to use steel framing in a 7-story hotel with 8,250 square feet per floor. What is the least expensive system of construction which will be permitted? _____

How much fire protection will be required on the lower-floor columns in this hotel? _____

What fire resistance rating will be necessary in the partitions around individual guest rooms? _____

What fire resistance rating is required for the exit stairway enclosures? _____

There is a 5'-wide pedestrian passage along one side of the site which the owner would like to develop as a shopping street. Can large glass display windows be used along this passage? _____ Can they be used along the street in front of the hotel? _____

7. In the space below, draw details of a) An appropriate floor-ceiling assembly for this hotel; b) An appropriate partition between guest rooms.

DESIGNING EXITWAYS

Here are some typical code excerpts concerning exitways in buildings other than single-family residences:

NUMBER: There shall be two (2) or more approved independent exitways serving every floor. Any room which exceeds 1500 square feet in floor area shall have at least two (2) egress doorways.

ARRANGEMENT: All required exitways shall be located so as to be visible and readily accessible with unobstructed access thereto, and so arranged as to lead directly to the street, or to an area of refuge with supplemental means of egress that will not be obstructed or impaired by fire, smoke, or other cause. Exitways shall be placed as remote from each other as practicable, and shall be arranged to provide direct access in separate directions from any point in the area served.

MAXIMUM LENGTH OF TRAVEL (measured from most remote point to nearest exitway)

Use Group	Length	Length with sprinkler system
Mercantile	100'	150'
Industrial	150'	250'
Business	200'	300'
Assembly	150'	200'
Institutional	100'	200'
Residential	100'	150'

DOORS: All doors shall be hung to swing in the direction of exit travel.

EXERCISE IN DESIGNING EXITWAYS

Indicate with circles on the following floor plans where you would locate exit stairways and exterior exit doorways in these buildings:

1. Nine-story apartment building, not sprinklered

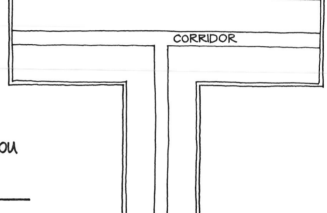

If this building had a sprinkler system, could you eliminate any exitways, and if so, how many?_____

2. Three-story school (use Group "Assembly"), not sprinklered

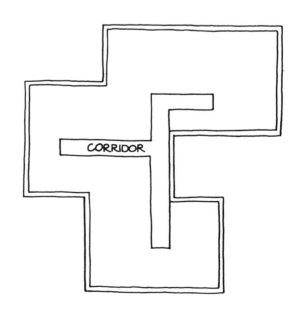

0   20   40   60 (feet)   _____name _____

3. Six-story department store, sprinklered

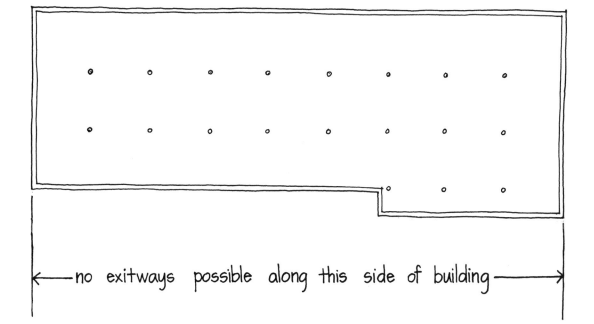

no exitways possible along this side of building

0   20   40   60 (feet)

MISCELLANEOUS CONSIDERATIONS IN SELECTING CONSTRUCTION SYSTEMS

Name one or more large-building construction systems which will be particularly suitable for each of the following situations:

1. Foundation conditions are poor, so dead weight of building must be minimized:

2. Building is in a Third-World country where steel is very expensive, but labor is cheap:

3. Frame must be erected during months of sub-freezing weather:

4. Construction must be extremely rapid:

5. Roof must span 150' without interior support:

6. Because of frequent labor difficulties, the number of separate trades needed to complete the building is to be minimized:

7. Client desires a building which looks and feels particularly solid, permanent, and reputable:

GETTING STARTED DESIGNING ALUMINUM EXTRUSIONS

Aluminum extrusions are produced with extreme precision, and with elegant possibilities for detailing. Some standard details for extruded aluminum curtain wall framing members are as follows:

BASIC SHAPE: Most sections are either a box shape or an I shape. The box shape has the advantage of being able to conceal fastening devices where it joins other framing members in a curtain wall.

SCREW FASTENINGS: The screw <u>port</u> allows screws to be driven into the ends of the section. This is especially useful for screwing one member to another in butted connections. The screw <u>slot</u> allows a screw to be driven perpendicular to the length of the section at any point. Screws may also be driven into <u>drilled</u> holes.

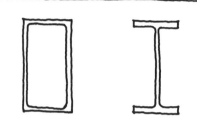

Screw Ports

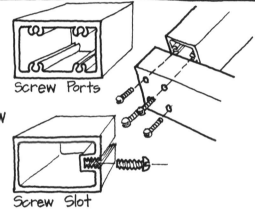

Screw Slot

SNAP-TOGETHER CONNECTIONS: Two parallel extrusions can sometimes be connected by means of snap-together details.

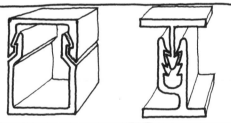

MOUNTING GLASS OR SPANDREL PANELS: Extruded neoprene gaskets are usually used to seal around glass or panels; they are snapped into slots in the aluminum extrusions. The stops which hold the glass or panels in place may be screwed to the main section, or snapped into place.

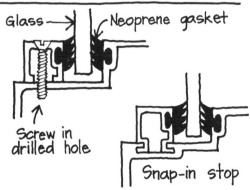

Glass → ⌐Neoprene gasket

Screw in drilled hole

Snap-in stop

DESIGNING ALUMINUM EXTRUSIONS

1. Shown below is a detail of a wood jamb and head for a fixed window. In the space to the right, draw the same detail using aluminum and neoprene extrusions. Include provisions for screwing the frame together at the corners.

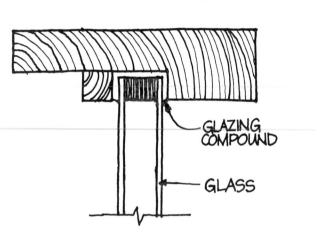

GLAZING COMPOUND

GLASS

4 (inches)

3

2

1

0

2. Outlined at the right is an aluminum curtain wall vertical mullion which supports two foam-core aluminum- clad spandrel panels. Complete the detail to include a screw-on exterior stop to hold the panels in place, neoprene extrusions to seal against the panels both inside and out, a snap-on cover over the exterior stop, and provisions for screwing the mullion to continuous horizontal mullions at each floor.

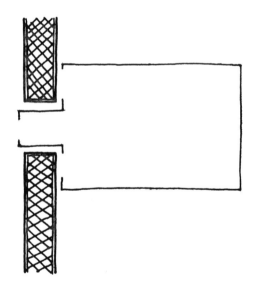

DETAILING OF FINISHES

On this section of an office building, outline a metal-and-glass curtain wall (you will be unable to show much detail at this scale), and detail the steel fireproofing, a suspended plaster ceiling, and a carpeted floor.

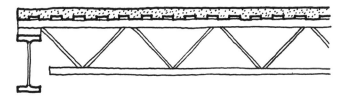

↑— CEILING LINE

0   1   2   3   4   (feet)

DETAILING OF FINISHES

Complete and label the details shown:

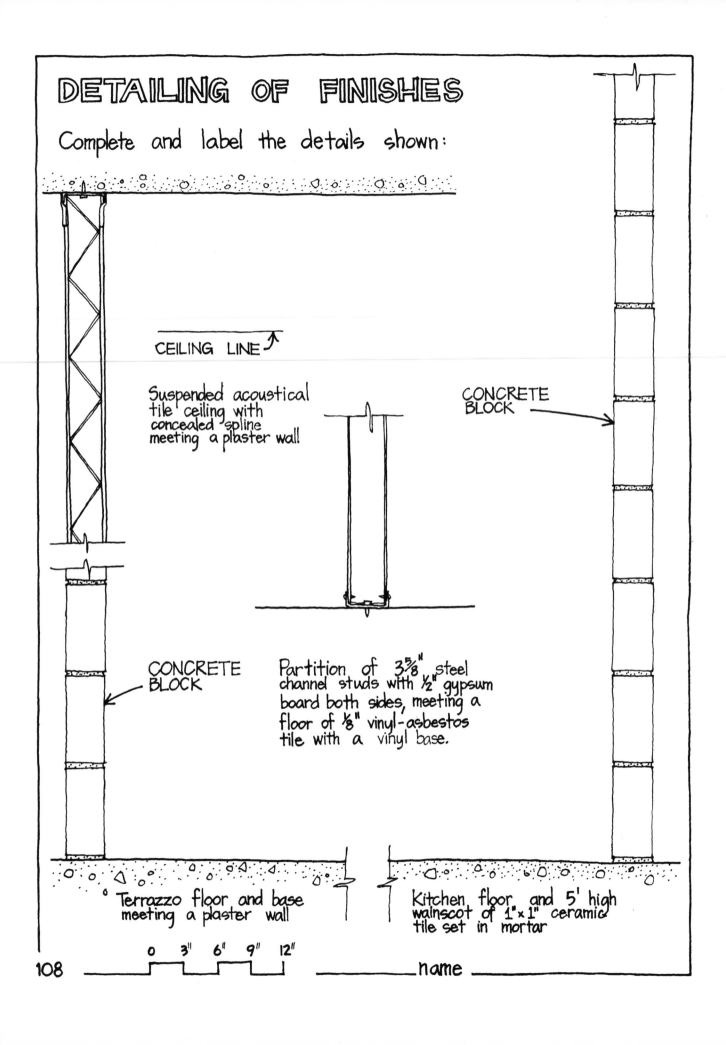

CEILING LINE

Suspended acoustical
tile ceiling with
concealed spline
meeting a plaster wall

CONCRETE
BLOCK

CONCRETE
BLOCK

Partition of $3\frac{5}{8}$" steel
channel studs with $\frac{1}{2}$" gypsum
board both sides, meeting a
floor of $\frac{1}{8}$" vinyl-asbestos
tile with a vinyl base.

Terrazzo floor and base
meeting a plaster wall

Kitchen floor and 5' high
wainscot of 1" x 1" ceramic
tile set in mortar

0   3"   6"   9"   12"

name

In the section below, draw foundation systems as indicated :

Bell Caisson

Precast concrete End-bearing pile

12" Concrete Bearing wall with 12" deep strip footing 4' below grade. Footing must support 6,000 lb/ft at a soil loading of 2 tons/ft^2

Cluster of sixteen wood friction piles 20' long, average diameter of 12"

GRADE

0   2   4   6   8   10   name

FIRM BEARING STRATUM

SLOPE RETENTION IN EXCAVATIONS

In the three excavations shown below in cross-section, draw slope-retention systems as specified.

1. Steel sheet piling supported by cross-lot bracing of steel wide-flange sections

2. Soldier piles and lagging supported by heavy wood rakers

3. Slurry wall supported by tiebacks

_____ name _____

DESIGN EXERCISE

A competition is being held for the design of the California Hot Rod Museum, to be built on a waterfront site in the Los Angeles area. The museum will house a changing display of customized automobiles of all types, from modified Model Ts to slingshot dragsters, from dune buggies to chromium-plated Rolls-Royces. Not more than 60 cars will be shown at any one time. Preparation and storage of cars will happen in an old warehouse around the corner — the museum is to be, simply, a sculpture gallery for automotive art. It needs only an entrance and lobby, toilets, a ticket counter, a small administrative office, and 40,000 square feet of display area.

The rules of the design competition require that you submit a combined site plan and ground floor plan, other floor plans as necessary, a cross-section, a perspective, a list of all major materials, and a typical exterior wall detail. Because you are entering the competition only a couple of days prior to the deadline, you have decided to do a rather simple, straightforward piece of architecture, and let the cars themselves be the focus of attention. All competition entries are to be checked for code compliance before judging.

On this sheet, draw the floor plans and cross-section of the building you have designed. Show column locations appropriate to the structural system you have selected, and show all necessary means of egress.

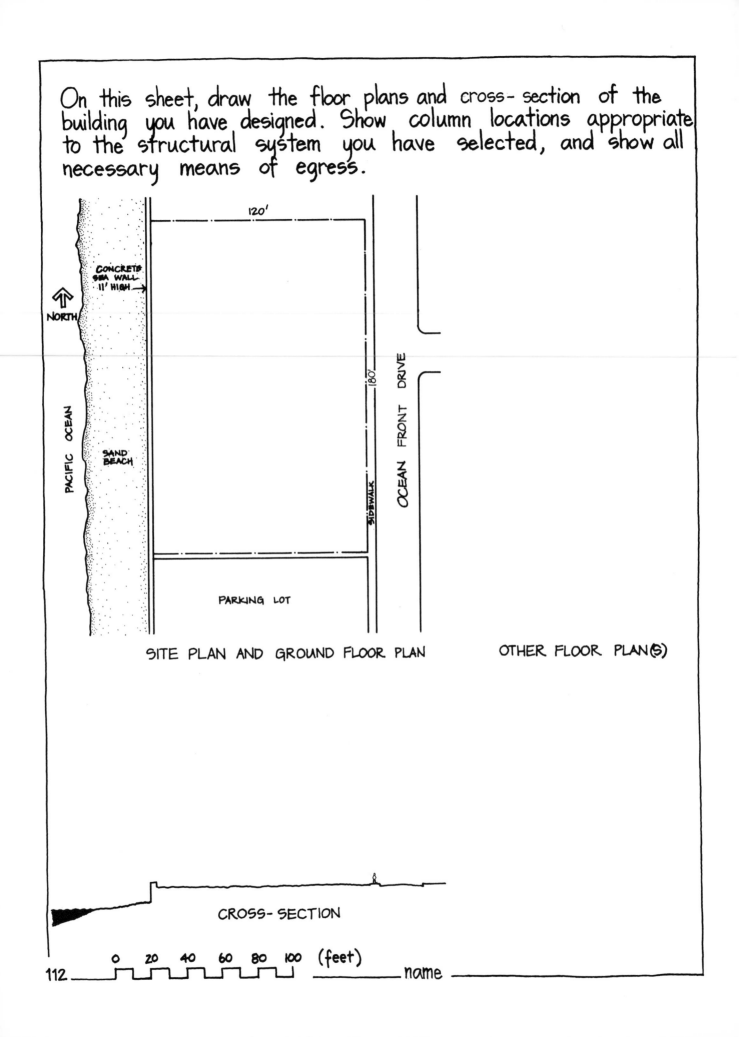

NORTH

PACIFIC OCEAN

CONCRETE SEA WALL 11' HIGH →

SAND BEACH

120'

180'

SIDEWALK

OCEAN FRONT DRIVE

PARKING LOT

SITE PLAN AND GROUND FLOOR PLAN

OTHER FLOOR PLAN(S)

CROSS-SECTION

0   20   40   60   80   100   (feet)

name

On this sheet, draw a perspective of the building as it is seen from eye level. A perspective of the interior might be especially appropriate.

List the major materials your building will require:

1. Structural system and type of construction as defined in building code:

2. Structural fireproofing:

3. Roofing system and roof insulation:

4. Exterior surface of walls:

5. Wall insulation:

6. Interior surface of walls:

7. Wall framing (if any:)

8. Interior partitions:

9. Finish floor material:

10. Finish ceilings:

11. Glass:

12. Frames for glass and exterior doors:

13. Stair treads:

14. Is the building sprinklered?

15. Hours of fire resistance:

Roof structure:

Upper-floor columns:

Floor structure:

Lower floor columns:

Partitions:

16. Entrance walk paving:

On this sheet, complete your entry by drawing a typical exterior wall section that shows how the materials you have selected are combined to make the building you have designed:

0   1   2   3   (feet)

TEACH YOURSELF TO BUILD

These exercises can only introduce you to the pleasures, potentials, and problems of building construction. But your further education in construction lies all around you, ready for the taking. Here are some suggestions:

1. Never pass by a building under construction without noting carefully what materials are being used, how they are being put together, and what result is being achieved. Completed buildings, regardless of age, are fully as valuable as sources of information on materials and techniques, if you develop the habit of looking closely. What do you like about a given building, and how was this result obtained? Where has the building failed (a leak, a sag, a crack, an unpleasant room, an ugly exterior) and why?

2. Skilled tradespeople are the finest source of information on their particular crafts. Watch how they work, and ask questions whenever you can. In most cases, a skilled worker is flattered that someone will take an interest in his/her artistry, and will be happy to talk. Even when you are the designer of a building that is under construction, listen carefully to what the workers have to tell you. Nine times out of ten they'll teach you something, and your next building will be the better for it.

3. Never spend only the time in a hardware store that it takes to make your purchase. Browse, and marvel at the human ingenuity that is distilled in the tools and building components you find there. Lumberyards, brickyards, quarries, even gravel pits are goldmines of information on building. Use all your senses to gather this information-- touch, smell, sound, sight. Become familiar with colors, odors, densities, roughnesses, patterns, and sounds of various materials. Develop a tactile "feel" that becomes a natural part of your design knowhow.

4. Read manufacturers' catalogs and literature. Send off to companies whose ads you see in architectural and engineering magazines for their literature, and start your own files of information. Tear out the free data cards in magazines and keep your mailbox full of technical information for weeks at a time merely by circling the numbers. Interrogate salespeople and representatives of building materials manufacturers and suppliers whenever you meet up with them. Learn to discriminate the genuine, durable, attractive products from the shabby imitations.

5. Look for summer and part-time jobs in construction, or in the offices of architects and engineers. Pester your employers to let you work in all facets of the job, both in the office and in the field.

6. Best of all _build_ with your own hands, even if it is just to patch cracked plaster or fix a wobbly chair. A garage, deck, or house addition is worth an advanced degree. Read the how-to books, do the design, order the materials, and do the work. Buy good tools (a solid, lifetime investment) and keep them sharp and clean. Feel the euphoria of each day's accomplishment and learning. Learn from your mistakes as well as your successes. Do better next time. Yes, there _will_ be a next time. Construction is habit forming.